Drumming & Dreaming

Drumming & Dreaming

Larry Spotted Crow Mann

Published by: CrowStorm Publishing™
Edited by: Nicole Sterling
Cover Art: Robert Peters & Robert Peters Jr.

ISBN: 1977660924
ISBN 13: 9781977660923

Foreword

In April of 2015, I was fortunate enough to have been invited to be a guest speaker at Haskell Indian Nations University in Kansas. It was for their 6th Annual Indigenous Empowerment Summit. It was an amazing week of inspirational stories, cultural resources, music, powwow, and traditional cuisine. A special thanks to Julia White Bull for making it possible for me to be there. I was thrilled to bear witness to hundreds of young Natives achieving academic greatness while maintaining strong ties to their culture.

The most honored moment was when I asked to do the opening prayer and song for Sunrise Ceremony. The Ceremony is conducted at the Sacred Medicine Wheel. This revered area of the Haskell Campus is where hundreds of Native children lost their lives due to abuse, neglect, and suicide during the Boarding School era.

Most of the graves are unmarked.

It was 5 A.M. when Student and Committee Leader of the Empowerment Summit, Chris Sindone, came to pick me up at the hotel. As we traversed the early morning roads of Laurence Kansas, Chris began giving me the layout for the morning events. I listened intently. Preparing for Ceremony is always a serious matter.

But what I've found in most Native communities, including my own; a bit of levity is often the first dose of *Medicine*.

This led to our subsequent discussion of whether Frybread taste better than Bannock. There is a lot of Tribal pride throughout United States and Canada concerning these two breads. So, we were both meticulous in laying out our case of our own personal preference, which I won't mention here. Chris is currently the Student Senate President at Haskell. His impartiality on such matters is crucial. In addition, Mr. Sindone being a New York Yankees fan, and I being a Boston Red Sox fan, led to further complications. We decided to drop the matter altogether.

When we arrived at the Sacred Medicine Wheel, the morning dew kissed the air, and the night had not yet surrendered its chill. I walked with Chris to gather wood for the Ceremonial Fire. Many other students and Haskell staff soon joined us for Ceremony. It was an honor to be there with these future Tribal leaders and faculty working so hard to make a difference. We formed a circle, took in the moment, and prayed in silence.

When the first flame of the Sacred Fire came forth, it reminded me of a new birth.

The crackling embers, and a bird off in the distance singing a beautiful song, spoke first. Father Sun slowly peaked. The Trees that edged the horizon, glinted a silhouette, emblazoned with a splendid, orange glow. The wetlands that border the Medicine Wheel, were patched with tall brindled reeds that danced in the gentle wind.

This was one of the most peaceful, Lovely, and serene moments I can recall.

Yet, I was standing in a place where; countless tears have fallen, cries for help were ignored, and the right to exist as a Native American was denied. The beauty and blessings of a new day were all around, and it merged in my heart with the great tragedy that befell all these innocent children.

I took out my Drum and began singing the Nipmuc Healing Song. The words are all in my *Algonquian* language. It brought to mind how language and story were forbidden to these young souls. And more than anything else, I wanted my prayers to convey a message of survival and resistance.

This is the same survival and resistance that I am, also, a product of. Our Elders tell us that, "We are the answer to someone's prayer; and someone's Dream."

What you are about to read are Indigenous Tales that never made it to the ears and hearts of countless children that it was meant for. So, may these Stories flow on the lips of the Wind and eternally Whisper in the Hearts of every Little Soul.

This is Your Book. These are Your Stories.

—◊—

Acknowledgments

I would like to give thanks to my Brother from the Passamaquoddy Nation, Roger Paul for passing on the story of *Matahqwas* and the *Birch Bark Canoe*. Your knowledge as a Culture Keeper, your kindness, and giving Spirit are immeasurable. To my cousin David Tallpine who helped with some of the Nipmuc language. Thank you for allowing the readers to hear our words and feel the story within Nipmuc Space.

I also want to acknowledge that some of the Stories in *Drumming & Dreaming* are with variations of the Telling from Nation to Nation (Including Nipmuc Bands) and are shared by Many other Tribes throughout the East. Some of the Tales, will be heard for the first time. And with that, Thank you to all the Story Tellers, Culture, and Language Keepers. The valiant work that you do keeps the pulse within our souls vibrant and ongoing. You inform the World of who we were and who we continue to be.

To all my colleagues and Indigenous writers, thank you for all that you do. Let's keep telling Our Stories!

Special shout out to Lisa Brooks (Abenaki) who did incredible work on our Nipmuc ancestor, probably the most famous, James the Printer. It's an honor, thank you, Lisa! Thank you, Robert Peters and Robert Peters Jr. for your wonderful artwork. You have surely captured the embodiment of this journey through your gift. Thank you, once again, to Nicole Sterling for editing this book. Your support and friendship has been invaluable during this process.

To my Mother, Aunts, Uncles, and Grandparents. Thank you for passing down the art of Story. Through your voices, laughter, and the many times of painful struggles, I have realized the honored mission bestowed upon me to keep the Story going. Thank You. To my Great Grandma, Lucy Vickers we've never met in this World, but you have, often, visited my dreams and told me of the Tears of the Cedar Tree. Kuttabatamish!

To my 4th Great Uncle Samuel Hazard who was known as the "Indian Doctor Hazard," connected to the Hatched Pond Nipmuc Reservation. He passed down cures and legends from skunk oil Medicine, to rattlesnake hearts to save a life. (That Story will be for another book.) Thank you for allowing me to carry a part of you.

To my Great Great Aunt Anna May Vickers who at 10 years old was taken from her home and sent to the Connecticut Industrial School for Girls. You are not forgotten.

To Konkontu (Crow), Kuttabatamish for these Ways. Thank you for letting me tell this Story through you. It's an honor, Netomp. To Mosq (Bear), Kuttabatamish for your Help. Tobacco down, Prayers Up.

There are numerous universities, schools, libraries, and other organizations that have shown me tremendous support, that I could never name them all. I deeply appreciate you all for taking this journey with me. Thank you for allowing the Voice of my Ancestors to traverse the ears of your students and in the halls of your establishments.

To all my children: Nathalie, Manixit, Mattawamp-Nantai, and Mattonas-Anoki; I Love you guys more than anything, and I hope I make you proud. To my Nipmuc People, we have seen joy and we have felt pain, But We Shall Remain. These are our Stories. May they bring us even closer together and continue to strongly build for the next generations to come.

To my sister Juaquina and my three Brothers: Troy, Charles, and Angel; through the good times, and not so good times, it's still has been wonderful to grow up with you. Thanks for always being there, Love you guys.

To all my friends, and relatives who have supported me, and, at times, kept me going through the vicissitudes of my life; Thank You!

Special thanks to all of the readers. I truly appreciate your support and I hope you enjoy *Drumming & Dreaming*.

And, to all the First Nations people throughout United States, Canada, and South America; I hope through my work that I have, in some way, carried your laughter, tears, joy, and pain so that the World may know and understand, just a little bit more about, who we are, and show that, all of us, as Human Beings, have a common bond. *Kuttabatamish* (Thank you, very much)

Introduction

Drumming & Dreaming is a collection of Algonquian tales of the Eastern Woodland Native Americans; primarily the Nipmuc Tribe. The Nipmucs are the original people of Worcester County, much of central New England, and beyond, stretching from Southern New Hampshire to Springfield and down into Northern Connecticut and Rhode Island.

To Native Americans, these Traditional Stories are Sacred. They give life and meaning to everything in the universe. They show us lessons of Love, courage, kindness, respect, humility, truth, and wisdom. We learn the skills to interact with our environment, as a living being, and codify those teachings within our own existence.

These legends also represent the unknown, Magic, and that things are not always as they seem. Sometimes, a tale is shared just for a good laugh. But at the very roots, it's all about the *Healing Power* that the message carries.

In Drumming & Dreaming, that Healing Power is called upon by Crow. He has suffered a great tragedy and cannot find his *Dream*. When

Bear sees his winged friend in distress, he comes to his aid. As you accompany Crow and Bear on this quest; the beauty, mystery, and wonder of Turtle Island mightily reveals itself.

Through the voice of Crow, and guidance of Bear, Mother Earth, once again, speaks in the language of the Indigenous People of North America.

As long as, We, the descendants of the First Peoples of North America are here, the Stories never die.
They live in us and through us.
If ever they become dormant, we have the power to revive them in that Ancient Voice, in which our Ancestors speak.
And through our Ancestor's voice, comes the authority, and authenticity to allow the Story to continue to be told.

Wutche Okasoh

Table of Contents

Foreword· v

Acknowledgments ·ix

Introduction · xiii

Kutche (The Beginning) · 1

Creation Story · 5

Nipmuc Legend of the Drum · 9

Matahqwas · 13

Sky Bear · 21

Round Dance Rabbit · 31

The Story of Matchemungqus· 37

Wild Cat Learns a Lesson · 47

Gift of the Strawberry · 53

The Three Sisters· 57

Tears of the Cedar Tree: A Love Story · · · · · · · · · · · · · · · 61

Mukkiah Weesug · 67

Corn Doll Woman · 73

Birch Bark Canoe · 77

Toad Woman of the Swamp· 79
Crow Challenges Hobomook · 89
How Crow Brought the Corn · 99

About the Author · 109

Kutche
(The Beginning)

*D*elicate morning mist hovered silently above Fresh Water Lake.

The warm Sun began to peak at its edge. The calm waters reflected streaks of purple, crimson, and patches of white from the sun-kissed clouds. Willows, Pines, and Chestnut Trees along the shore, stretched out their impressive shadows across the pond. A family of Wood Thrush were sprinkled about the Trees, singing a soft melody.

A huge Trout made the clouds and Trees shimmer, when he broke through the surface, and gulped down a water bug. A giant black paw quickly thrusted down.

It emerged with the Trout hooked into its large claws. Bear began to feast on his catch, as he stood waist deep in Fresh Water Lake.

The sandy shores retreated to green, fertile Earth. A trail lead through the thick Forest. Rustling and strange noises were coming from a thicket nearby.

Bear quickly turned toward the Forest. He dropped his meal back into the water, and went to explore. Bear parted his way through a thicket to see what the noise was in the woods. It was Crow. Crow's feathers were ruffled. He swayed sided to side, as if about to fall over. He looked confused, as he wobbled in circles. Crow was talking to himself in jumbled sentences.

Bear shouted, "Crow! What are you mumbling about?"

"I am trying to remember that Dream," said Crow.

"What dream?" asked Bear.

"That is the problem, I do not know what World this is. Are you Dream?"

Bear looked at his feet, then hands, "I do not know if I am Dream," he replied. Bear turned his head side to side, studying Crow and asked, "What happened to you, Crow?"

"The last I remember, I was flying from the far side of the Mountains. There was a great Storm. All of my Clan died. My Magic left with them. I need to transform to the Dream World—to find them. Please tell me Bear, are you Dream?"

"I said, I do not know," replied Bear.

Crow's eyes looked heavy and he lowered his beak.

Bear looked upon him with sorrow. Bear rubbed his chin, cleared his throat and said, "Crow, maybe, I can help. Help you find Dream."

"It's hopeless Bear. Without my family, my powers have faded."

Bear looked around, "Wait, I think I know where your Dream is."

"*Where?*" *Asked Crow, with excitement.*

"*It is in the Story,*" *said Bear.*

"*The Story?*" *Crow replied.*

"*Rest your weary feathers and tell me a story, Crow.*"

"*I cannot remember any stories,*" *replied Crow.*

"*Think about something. Something to remind you,*" *Bear urged.*

"*I cannot. My heart is much troubled,*" *said Crow.*

Bear thought for a moment, "Yes, yes that is it, Crow. How about a sound? The first sound you remember?"

Crow lifted his head, "Sound?...Yes, yes it was the beat. The sound of my Heartbeat."

Bear reached underneath a Blackberry bush. He picked up his Drum.

He looked around on the ground, sniffed and kicked up some underbrush. "Where did I put that Drum beater?" He asked himself.

"*No problem.*" *He said. Bear picked up a small Oak branch. He ate the leaves off.*

"*Listen,*" *he said as he began beating the Drum; using the branch for a Drumstick.*

"*This is like the sound of your Heartbeat. Now, let that sound bring ease and memory to your mind.*" *He told Crow.*

Crow began to relax and listen.

Bear continued to Drum and then looked back toward the Lake, thinking about all those delicious fish waiting to be eaten. "Okay, Crow, now try. Try to find your Dream."

"Yes, Bear. But where should I look first?"

"Let us start, at the beginning of all things."

"The beginning?" Crow asked.

"Yes, the beginning. The beginning of Turtle Island. Can you remember how we all came here, Crow?"

"Yes. When I was very young, I sat on a Willow branch. Below, an old Nipmuc Man was telling children the Creation Story. It went like this."

—⁂—

Creation Story

They say that, we Nipmuc started as Sky Beings, without form, living with Manitoo in the Great Darkness.

Out of the darkness, *Manitoo* (The Great Mystery) fashioned *Mishe-Toonupasug* (Great Turtle) as a symbol of His wisdom, patience, and old age. And from the sweat of His hands, He made a very large ball of Water, to be the home for the Turtle. In the Water, He made all sorts of life, some for the Turtle to feed on. As Mishe-Toonupasug became larger and larger, her back rose above the surface of this giant ball of Water. As it rose up, she brought on her back the soil and stones that were at the bottom. This created the First Island –'*Turtle Island.*' Small Plants began to spring up on her back. But it was cold and dark. So, Manitoo made the Sun to give warmth and light. He then divided the light in half with the darkness, to give Turtle Island balance and harmony. He sprinkled Stars into the night Sky to ensure that all was not dark, and as the reminder of the *Path*, in which we have come. Grandmother Moon joined the Stars, and her Cycles would represent the Nature of Life. The Giant Turtle's back is marked with *13 Squares* for *13 Moons*; to signify these *Life Cycles* and Turtles Island's cycle of passing around the Sun.

With the warmth of the Sun, the Plants grew larger. Then came giant Trees, Insects and Birds; then the Animals. Then the *Sky Beings* came; which is the *Spirit* of the *Human Being.* Manitoo first put Sky Beings inside of Stone. But Manitoo was not pleased. He then put Sky Beings in a Tree. Still not satisfied, he tried Water, then Plants, then Animals. Eventually, Sky Beings were put into everything. Finally, Manitoo decided to make a new thing to place Sky Beings in: Human Beings, or the Two Legged.

And when the Two Legged arrived, they knew that *All Are Related* and had much to learn from all the Living Things around them. And so, our journey of Being Human is connected to all Life. Our Path of this Life is represented by the *Four Fires,* kindled by the *Four Winds.*

Wutchepwosh the Eastern Wind, kindles the Fire of the East, representing the beginning. Our journey, as it starts, on Turtle Island.

Sowansh the Southern Wind, sparks forth the Fire of the South, signifying the time of innocence, learning, growing, and sharing.

Nanumit the Grandfather, the ancient Northern Wind blows forth the cold Fire of the North, representing wisdom, patience, and passing on of our ancient Stories.

Paponetin the Western Wind, Wind of Endless Spirts ignites the eternal Fire of the West, honoring the place of Dreams, Spirit, and the Endless Circle of Creation.

—m—

"Well done, Crow. Have you found your Dream?" Asked Bear.
"No. But I very much enjoyed sharing that with you, Bear," replied Crow.
"Good, then tell me more. Think of another one," said Bear.
"You spoke of the Heartbeat. I believe I recall one of that sort," said Crow.

Nipmuc Legend of the Drum

Back during the beginning of Creation, the Nipmuc Men were having trouble getting along.

They bickered over almost everything. With all that arguing and inability to agree on much, they lacked balance. The Clan Mothers of the villages stepped in to bring reason and calmness to the situation. It worked for a short while. But once again, the Clan Mothers would have to intervene. The Men could not seem to stop the endless quarrelling. The Nipmuc Women got fed up and gave them a sharp and final warning, "If you don't stop all this fighting with each other, we will leave!"

Well, the Men didn't stop fighting and the Women did as they said. All the Women of the villages left. As they walked away, they proclaimed, "We will not return until you find peace and harmony amongst yourselves." The Men were unhappy that the all the Women left, but they did not know how to stop fighting.

Finally, they all set off to the woods and prayed to Manitoo, the Great Spirit. They cried out- "Oh Manitoo, please help us, help us find harmony!" The Men prayed and fasted for days and days. After more time had passed, a great storm came. The Sky darkened and a gray mist came over the Forest. Howling, buzzing wind, forceful rain, and mighty thunder crackled all around. Branches of Trees, leaves, and debris hurled around with blinding force.

A powerful blue lightning bolt hit a huge Oak Tree near some of the Men. It knocked the Tree down, close to the bottom of the trunk, and left a perfectly round stump. Another vigorous lightning bolt hit the inside, making a hole in the part of the stump that was left. Out of the haze, a glowing, white object appeared. As it got closer, it revealed to be a huge, gleaming, White Deer. It trotted forth, but seemed to float amid the chaotic storm, untouched and unharmed. The Deer crossed paths with one of the Men and said, "I understand you have great trouble among you. I will now leave you something to bring you peace and harmony. But, you must always show it respect and honor. It is powerful and Sacred Medicine. Let your Hearts guide you." In that moment, the Deer made a final gallop and leaped down into the smoldering Tree. When the Man ran over to it, all he saw was the beautiful white hide of the Deer left behind. As the other Men ran around to see what was going on, he explained to them what had happened: "The Deer Spirit is in the Tree!" he shouted. The Men looked inside with awe. They were overtaken by a commanding sense of peace, Love, and joy. The raging Storm had ceased. All in the Forest had gone completely silent. Except for one sound. As the Nipmuc Men leaned into the Tree and marveled at the beauty of the Deer hide, they heard the sound of a Heartbeat pulsating inside.

That same Nipmuc Man outstretched the beautiful, white Deerskin over the base of what was left of the Tree. The Man said a Prayer and placed Tobacco over it. He picked up one of the broken sticks around him and said, "I will follow my Heart." He began tapping on the hide in the same way they heard the pulsing beat from the inside. He began singing an Honor Song. Then another Man grabbed a stick and began to sing with him. And another Man picked up a branch and did the same. Soon, all the Men were singing together in harmony and balance, on the top of the deer hide. They knew Creator had given them something Sacred. The Heart Beat of the Earth, they called it. They went back to the village and proclaimed a great gift has been bestowed on them. And when the Women saw that the Men were at peace and harmony, they returned to the village. But they gave the Men another stern warning. The Clan Mothers said, "Creator has giving you something precious and Sacred, The Heart Beat of the Mother. We will watch over the Drum to ensure you Honor this Gift." Even today, Women stand around the Drum while it is being played, as the protectors of the Sacred Drum.

—⟶⟶—

"Very good, Crow. The more Stories you share, the more I believe, you will find your Dream."

Matahqwas

Long ago, it was this way. Before the Human Beings were here on Turtle Island, Creator made the Animals first.

One of the Animals was Rabbit, or as we say, *Matahqwas*. Matahqwas didn't look like he does today, back then. He was handsome, lean, and tall enough to look a large Moose eye to eye. He had a nice round face and had tiny ears. What's more, Matahqwas had a long, beautiful, and fluffy tail that he was very proud of.

Because Matahqwas was so handsome, he thought he was Creator's favorite of them all. He would tease and make fun of all the other Animals saying how beautiful he was, and how ugly the others were.

"Bear, look at you!" he laughed heartedly, "You are so furry and smelly. And you don't even have a proper tail."

Bear replied, "Oh Matahqwas, do not be so harsh."

Matahqwas just laughed and pointed some more. Then, he turned his attention to Moose.

"Moose!" He shouted with a laugh, "What was Creator thinking when he made you? You have those large, silly things growing out of your head. But, I must say, Moose, the sight of you makes me laugh, greatly."

Moose was very upset and said, "Oh Matahqwas, leave me alone."

Matahqwas said, "Don't blame me, Moose, because you do not have such a long beautiful tail as mine, or nice small ears that are snug to my head. Surely, it is only because I am the favorite of Manitoo."

One day, Creator called for all the Animals to come to a meeting. He had something very important to tell them. From every part of the Forest, Swamps, and Mountains; every creature came together in a great Circle: Deer, Beaver, Snake, Hawk, Otter, Owl, Squirrel, Spider, Bat, Wolf, and on and on, it went. And, of course, the Rabbit, Matahqwas.

Manitoo spoke, "Thank you, all my Animal Beings, Flying and Crawling Ones, for coming to this Gathering. I have a very important message to tell you all. I am going to make a new creature," Creator said, "It will be different from all of you." All the Animals, Birds, and Crawlers turned to each other and chatted softly around the great Circle. Each one was trying to guess what was to come.

Creator said, "These new creatures will be called 'Human Beings.'"

All the chatter stopped as Creator went on, "Yes, they are to be called Human Beings. They will not be like you, for they will be very fragile and need your help. They will need you to teach them how to hunt, plant, build, and survive on Mother Earth. Could you all help them with that?"

"Yes, of course, we will help them Manitoo!" Shouted all the creatures.

"Kuttabatamish," said Creator. "I knew I could always depend on you all. But there is one more important thing you must know," he added, "The Human Beings frighten very easy, so please be gentle and do not scare them." The Animals all agreed not to scare the disadvantaged Human Beings.

Just as Creator said, the Human Beings arrived. They were stumbling around, lost, and confused. They didn't know Water from a Tree, or a Stone from a Loon. They were going to need a lot of help, indeed.

Matahqwas did not like them, right away. He said they were ugly and useless. "Why would Creator make such an ugly thing?" He asked himself.

Matahqwas decided he wasn't going to do as Creator asked. And everywhere he would see a Human Being, he was going to scare them. As the Humans were wandering around trying to figure out the World, Matahqwas hid behind a large rock. Just as Human Being was walking by, he jumped out and yelled, "RAAH!"

The Human Being ran off into the brush, trembling and curled into a ball.

Matahqwas laughed and went in search of another one to frighten. He saw another Human Being walking down a narrow path. Matahqwas concealed himself behind a Pine Tree as the Man approached. "RAAH!" He shouted. The Human Being was so terrified that he jumped high off the ground, with his feet running in the air. When he hit the ground, he fled down the path and cried out, "Manitoo! Manitoo! Help! Matahqwas is scaring me!"

Creator heard the Two-Legged cry. Manitoo was very upset with Matahqwas. Creator shouted, his voice like thunder, "Matahqwas!" Matahqwas knew he was in big trouble. He ran. He searched desperately

for a place to conceal himself. He scurried about, here and there, looking for a place to hide. He tried the bank of a River, then a bush, then
next to the side of a Stone. None of those places were safe enough, he
thought. Then his eyes spotted a large, felled Oak Tree. Matahqwas
darted towards it. He squeezed his long body into the hollowed-out
Tree. The top of his head peaked out one end and his long, fluffy tail
hung out of the other side.

Creator asked many of the Animals if they had seen Matahqwas. But
not one creature knew where he was. Matahqwas remained hidden in the
log and dared not come out. Numerous days later, Bear was out picking
Berries from a bush.

"Hey, Bear!"

Bear looked up and around to see who had called him. He did not see
anyone.

Bear resumed picking his delicious Berries.

"Hey Bear, down here!" The voice said.

It was Matahqwas, calling from inside the log.

"Matahqwas?" Asked Bear. "Manitoo is looking for you, what are you
doing in that Tree?"

"I have been hiding from Manitoo," he said. "But now, I am stuck inside. Get me out of here, Bear!" Shouted Matahqwas.

Bear looked around and said, "I don't know about this, Matahqwas.
Manitoo is angry with you. I wish not to be involved in your troubles."

Matahqwas had to strain just to speak, and said, "You better do as I say, Bear, or I will tease you even more, next time."

Bear said, "Alright, alright, I will help."

Bear stood tall over the center of the felled Tree. He closed his paw tight, raised it high to the sky. He pounded down as hard as he could. The Tree did not split. This time, Bear put both his paws tightly together. He pounded again. But still the Tree did not break. Bear was strong, but the Oak was stronger. Bear asked himself, 'How can I get Matahqwas out?'

He looked at the long, fluffy tail of Matahqwas, which was resting outside the log.

"Don't you worry, Matahqwas! I have a way to get you out," he declared.

Bear grasped a hold of his tail and he began to pull, but Matahqwas did not budge. So, he pulled, tugged, and pulled some more.

Just as he gave another forceful heave, the Rabbit's tail snapped off.

Bear fell backwards and tumbled to the ground with the long beautiful tail still in his paws. Matahqwas was still stuck. He could not see on either side, or the rear, and had no idea what had just happened to his prized possession: his tail.

"What is going on, back there?" He asked Bear.

Bear quickly got to his feet. "Nothing, nothing is wrong," he replied, as he looked nervously at the tail.

"Then, get me out of this Tree!" Matahqwas shouted.

Bear quickly hurled the tail far off into the woods. Bear wiped his paws and said, "Let me try from the other side."

Bear came around to where his head was sticking out.

He did not want to yank him by the neck, fearing his head would go the same way as his tail. Instead, he gently put one claw behind both of his tiny ears.

He began to pull him forward, by the ears. Matahqwas did not move, but his ears started to stretch.

And as he pulled, his ears stretched more and more. His ears stretched way, way, way out, and Bear kept pulling. Finally, Matahqwas broke free. But because he was in the Tree for such a long time, his body got pushed down and hunched over. However, his feet remained the same size. Some of the other animals were laughing at him. One of them was Moose, "Look it, look it Matahqwas!"

Matahqwas looked around and was wondering what did they find so amusing.

He went over to the stream to look at himself in the Water. He saw that his ears were now very long and dangling to the ground. He yelled, "No! How could this be?! Where are my beautiful small ears?! These are horrible!" He reached around to feel for his tail, but there was only a stub of what used to be his tail.

He cried out, "Manitoo! Help me, help me! My tail is gone! And my ears, my ears are stretched out!"

Creator said, "Matahqwas, I asked you to help me, and not scare the Human Beings. But you did not listen. And because you did not listen to me, I will leave you with those long ears, to better hear me next time. Matahqwas, you have been very boastful with your long tail. So, now I will leave you with this small one, so you won't be such a show off. The little tail will be a reminder to be thankful for what you have."

Creator then told Matahqwas there was one last consequence of his actions.

"And from now on, when you see a Human Being, they will not be afraid of you. *You* will be the one that will be afraid of them."

—⚏—

Bear laughed, "I was in that Story." He scratched his head, sniffed his shoulder and took a more serious tone, "Matahqwas is wrong you know, I do not 'smell.'"

"Bear," said Crow, "I am sharing the Story and—"

"But Crow," pleaded Bear, "I surely do not —"

"Bear!" Crow interrupted, "I have another story coming to my Heart. I believe it will please you."

Sky Bear

Long ago, after a journey from an unknown place, the first *Mosq* (Bear) walked into the Nipmuc Homeland.

It was a very large female Bear. She was pregnant with twin cubs. She found the Nipmuc land to be beautiful with all sorts of food, bountiful Lakes and Rivers, filled with plenty of fish. There were plenty of Trees, grasses, Berries, pretty flowers, nuts, and Plants, everywhere. She decided to stay and make this their home. Shortly, thereafter, her twin cubs were born. After nursing them for a little while, she needed to give them other foods.

Being new to this wonderful place, she was not sure what to feed her twins.

So, one she fed only fruits, nuts, and grass. The other she feed only fish and meat. The twins loved one another, dearly, and enjoyed challenging each other in all sorts of games. They were destined to be great leaders. Both cubs grew very strong, and rapidly. Soon, they began to change from each other. The cub that ate fruits, nuts, and grasses was very calm, and had a good Heart. When he ate, he was very delicate and neat with his food; gently picking Berries off a bush, one by one. He took his time in seeing the World.

The Bear cub that ate only meat and fish, also had good Heart. But he was always focused on protecting his Brother and Mother. He was very energetic, eager to get the things he wanted. His goal in life was to be the best and strongest Warrior ever. He also enjoyed fighting. His mother named him, Rough Minded Bear. And his Brother became known as, Gentle Minded Bear. The two Brothers began to disagree and bicker about everything. Although they still cared for each other, they took separate paths into Nipmuc Land. Each Bear formed their own powerful Clans. Gentle Minded Bear formed the Clan of thoughtfulness, Love, compassion, and laughter. Rough Minded Bear created the Clan of courage, strength, fierceness, and hunting skills. Each Bear Clan ruled over Nipmuc Land. They were the biggest, and one of the most powerful, creatures around.

Just as when they were Bear cubs, they were very competitive.

Each clan wanted to be the best at what they did and they constantly battled each other. During games of bravery and strength, the Rough Minded Clan won. During games of intelligence, accuracy and wisdom, the Gentle Minded Clan won. They were almost evenly matched in their expertise, but neither wanting to say who was the best.

After some time had passed, the Two-Legged creatures, the Nipmucs, were brought onto Mother Earth by the Great Spirit. When they arrived into Nipmuc Land, it was a beautiful, wondrous, and a plentiful place. But it also had many dangers and challenges for the Human Beings, who were last to arrive on Turtle Island.

In fact, the Nipmucs were having a very hard time surviving. They noticed the Bear Clans, and how powerful, lively, and plentiful their lives were.

One day, a young Nipmuc Man who Loved to Drum and sing songs, began observing the Rough Minded Bear Clan. He saw what great hunters, fishermen, and fighters they were. He wanted to learn from them.

The Nipmuc Man timidly approached Rough Minded Bear Chief, and said, "Greetings, Netomp. I noticed what a great hunter, warrior, and fishermen you are. Could you teach me so my Two-Legged people can survive?"

The Bear Chief gave the Nipmuc Man a stern look and said, "You should be ashamed of yourself, right now. Before you ask for something, you should have something to give."

The Man said, "But I have nothing to give." Bear thought for a moment and said, "What is that you are holding?"

"This is my Drum," said the Nipmuc Man.

"Okay Human Being, if you play me a song, I will teach you."

The Man agreed, and sang:

"Hey ya hey- I pray Rough Minded Bear teaches me the Ways- Hey ya hey- Hey ya hey- I pray Rough Minded Bear teaches me the Ways- Hey ya hey!"

Rough Minded said, "Yes, yes, it is good. The beating of the Drum makes my blood rush like the River after a Storm, or like the call of battle. Yes, I like it very well. But listen, Two Legged," the Bear said, "I can teach you, but there is something else you must do."

"Yes, tell me," the Man asked, "What would you have me do?"

Bear continued, "I have a twin Brother. He is the leader of the Gentle Minded Clan. We have been locked in battle for many, many Moons to see who has the best Clan. Each of us possesses secrets and powers of this land that the other does not have. But if I knew his secrets of the land, we could beat them. I will teach you to be the greatest hunter ever. But you must first go to my Brother's Clan and ask him to teach you the ways of the Gentle Minded Clan."

"I will do as you ask," said the Nipmuc Man. Just as the Man was about to run off to carry out his task, Bear stopped him by putting his huge paw on his shoulder. Bear said, "Hear these words. You must not tell him I asked you to do this. You will tell him that you want to learn all his ways. Once you have learned all his secrets, you bring the knowledge back to us. Then, I will teach you our ways."

The Nipmuc Man nervously looked at Rough Minded Bear, careful not make eye contact. He then glanced at the huge paw that covered his shoulder with claws that reached halfway down his chest. The Nipmuc Man nodded and said 'yes.' He was fearful about his task, but felt it was worth it to learn such great skills of survival.

He walked for a few days and made it to the Gentle Minded Clan. He went to the Gentle Mind Bear Chief and said, "Greetings, Netomp. I see you have great knowledge of all the plant Medicines, grasses, fruits, Trees, and the Insect World. You show great patience, smarts, and wisdom, when doing things. My people are new to Turtle Island and it is a dangerous place. Could you teach me all the ways of the Plant Medicines, the Trees, and which Berries to eat?"

Gentle Minded Bear looked at him and said, "Greetings, Netomp. But *you* are being ill mannered, right now. You have come asking for something without offering something, first."

The Nipmuc Man said, "I am sorry, but I have nothing to give."

"What is that you are holding?" Gentle Minded Bear asked.

"This is my Drum."

The Bear said, "Well then, sing me a song. If I like it, I will teach you."

The Man began singing a song.

"Hey ya hey- I pray Gentle Minded Bear teaches me the Ways- Hey ya hey- Hey ya hey- I pray Gentle Minded Bear teaches me the Ways- Hey ya hey!"

He sang it over and over. Gentle Minded Bear said, "Very good, Netomp, very good. Your singing is like having Sparrows for earrings, I like it very well. I will teach you. But because of what I will teach is very special, I need you to do one more thing for me."

"Yes, I will do as you ask." The Nipmuc Man replied.

"Once I teach you everything," Gentle Minded Bear said, "Go to my Brother and ask to learn his ways. Do not say I told you to do so. Once you learn, come back and teach us."

The Man said, "Yes."

Bear taught him everything they knew about Plant Medicine, Trees, the Insect World, and how to be patient and wise. Once he learned all the secrets of Gentle Minded Clan, the Man changed. His senses were stronger than ever. The World was more vibrant.

The Nipmuc Man returned to the village of Rough Minded Clan and said, "I have learned all the ways of Gentle Minded Clan."

Rough Minded Bear replied, "Good, tell me all that you know, then I will teach you all that I know."

The Nipmuc Man taught him all the Teachings of the Gentle Minded Clan he had learned. The Bear was much pleased. Then Rough Minded Bear taught the Man how to hunt, fish, be strong, and face danger with unbelievable courage.

Then as promised, the Nipmuc Man went back and showed Gentle Minded Bear what he learned. Gentle Minded Bear was very pleased learning the ways of his Brother Rough Minded Bear.

Once both Clans possessed the Sacred knowledge of the other, their bodies began to change. The Bears became larger, wiser, and heavier. So heavy, that when they walked, their paws would sink in the Earth and shake the ground.

The Nipmuc Man who held the Sacred knowledge of both Clans became a powerful Pau Wau. When he would Drum, the sound could penetrate the World of Dreams and Spirits.

The Bears resumed their competitions. Both Clans were surprised that now they were evenly matched, in ALL of the contests. Now, there were no more differences among them. The twin Brother Bear Chiefs were frustrated. They still wanted to compete and outdo each other's Clan. One of them thought of a new contest to try to see who was better.

They went further in the Forest. They searched out the largest and tallest Tree they could find. They came across an enormous white Pine

Tree. It was the tallest Tree in the Forest. So tall, the green branches stretched into the Sky and almost touched the Sun. One of the twins said, "Look at what I can do. Even though I am heavy, I can reach up very high and scratch my claws deep in this pine. Much higher than you, Brother," he added.

The other Bear said, "No, you cannot." He declared, "I can scratch much higher, watch this!"

And so, another competition emerged: to see who could scratch their huge claw marks the highest up unto this massive Tree. Higher and higher, up the Tree they climbed, trying to see who could scratch the highest point. Up, up, they went. Because they were twins, nobody could tell them apart, as they got further up the limbs.

They climbed and scratched, clawed and scaled up the giant Tree, into the dark of night. There were Bears on the ground that began to yell to them to be careful, and that they were going too high up. Some just wanted them to come back down. They were so far up, that the large black Bears appeared as dots from down below. After much time, and lots of scratching, the Bears were reaching the top. The twins scrambled as fast as they could to try and reach the tip first.

As one Bear lunged out, he began to slip. The other Bear reached out and shouted, "Brother, I will catch you, do not fall!"

He gave a great effort to grab hold of him, but he still was slipping away. As his Brother began to fall back away from the Tree; he reached out even further to try and save him. But as he did, he fell too. But as this twin started to fall, he crashed into one of the large, green branches. The branch cradled his huge body. The limb bent way back under the weight. Then, it whipped forward and shot him deep into the night Sky.

As the other twin began to fall to the Earth, he was propelled far, far up into the Stars. The twin who was falling towards the Earth, came charging down at great speed. His large body crashed to the Earth with such force, it went right down, below the ground and in between two Mountains. The Earth turned black at the place where he fell. The place where he fell is now known as '*Tantasqua.*'

The other Bear become stuck in the Sky, amongst the Moon and Stars.

And he became known as '*Pawkunnawaw,*' or Sky Bear.

All the Bears were sad for this loss. For one twin was lost below, and the other above. To mourn the loss of the Bear who fell at Tantasqua, all the Bears took scrapings of the Black Earth and painted themselves black. The Pau Wau came and consoled them and then covered himself with the black paint. The Pau Wau sang songs of mourning and reminded them they all have the *Medicine* and gifts of each other. Together, they looked up into the night Sky.

What we call today, as the North Star, is the top of that great White Pine Tree that Gentle Minded Bear and Rough Minded Bear climbed up, so long ago. And, now, *Pawkunnawaw* (Sky Bear) continues to circle it, forever looking for his twin Brother. With each passing season, Sky Bear looks in a different direction hoping to find him. Sky Bear is what some call *The Big Dipper.* The White Pine Tree became the place where there are no differences, a place to be One and united together, forever.

And because all the Bears had the Sacred Medicine of the other Clans, they were, indeed, powerful. They now possess abilities they have not yet realized. The Bears decided to pause all competition. And to honor these two great leaders, one Bear said, "I will fast one day." Another Bear said, "Well, I will fast two days." Another Bear said, "I will fast for a whole week." Soon all the Bears decided to fast until the cold wind has blown to the North and Spring arrives. The Bears said, "These were our leaders, one gone to the Sky and one in the Earth."

And the Nipmuc Man, who carried the knowledge of both Clans became very powerful and wise. He was very content to have the courage and hunting skills of Rough Minded Bear, and also the knowledge of plant Medicines, fruits, Insect World, and wisdom of Gentle Minded Bear. He told all the people of Nipmuc what had happened. In times of mourning, he would bring his people to Tantasqua and they would paint their faces with the black Earth, left by the Bear leader. He informed his people there was much to be learned from the Bear Nations.

The twin that fell to the Earth, teaches us about fasting, sacrifice, sharing, the connection of the living and Spirit World, and respect for all things. The twin that is fixed in the Sky, teaches us about resilience, patience, observation, courage, and Love. The Pau Wau was very thankful and took out his Drum and began to sing, "Ya, way, No, Ya, Gentle Minded - Rough Minded, I cannot tell them apart, Gentle Minded - Rough Minded, they are both in my Heart."

—⋙—

"Yes, *Kuttabatamish, Crow!*" said Bear. "My Mother told this story many times, when I was young. It has been so long since I have heard it. *Kuttabatamish.*"

"You are most welcome, Bear," he said, as he fanned out his feathers, "I can recall another one. Listen."

Round Dance Rabbit

This happened long ago, during the time of the Melting Moon Ceremony that occurs under the Moon of March and April.

Rabbit, or in our language, *Matahqwas*, was getting ready for a big Melting Moon dance and feast. He had a birch bark basket with some food, games, and hand Drum. He was thinking of some good ole songs to sing.

It was a long, cold winter and not everyone was thinking about the celebration. *Pussough*, or Bobcat, had a tough time finding food throughout the cold months. Now that the ice and snow was melting, he was hoping to have better luck. That is when he saw Matahqwas with his basket of food, Drum, and other goods.

"Ah, a tasty meal has been put before me," said Pussough.

The big Cat leaped out in front of the Rabbit, "Now, you are mine!" He shouted.

Rabbit cried, "Please do not eat me! Here, would you like some tasty acorns?"

"No! I want you," replied Pussough.

"How about a nice hunk of corn cake with dried Berries? And a bowl of fresh Maple sap, that is so sweet, to wash it down?" Matahqwas fretfully inquired.

"No, and no, I want to eat *you*. You are the taste I crave," said Pussough as he showed his large fangs. "Now, do not run away, my claws are sharp and I am faster than you, Matahqwas!"

Matahqwas said, "Very well, but please, I have one request before you eat me. I was on my way to Melting Moon celebration and now I will not be able to attend. I wanted to hear a Round Dance song. I will let you eat me, I will not run. All I ask, is you sing a Round Dance song on the Drum. When the song is over, you may eat me."

Pussough scratched his chin, twitched his nose and asked, "I sing, and you do not run? And when the song is done, I can eat you?"

"Yes, Pussough, yes. That is our deal," said Matahqwas.

Pussough grabbed the hand Drum from the basket. He beat the Drum three times and said, "The song is over, time to eat you."

"Wait!" Shouted Matahqwas, "A Round Dance song is much longer. And it *must* go four times through, to honor the Four Winds. If this is not done, Nanumit, the *Cold Wind of the North*, could not return and welcome his little Brother, Napatin, the *Spring Wind of the East*. Surely, you don't want that, seeing what a hard time you had during the time of snow."

Pussough snarled, "Quiet! I know of these things you speak."

"You do?" Asked Matahqwas, with a look of surprise.

The big Cat growled again, "Matahqwas, you talk too much. You are chattier than Crow."

Pussough began to sing, again. As he did, Matahqwas danced in a small Circle. When Pussough started the next *Round*, to honor the direction, Matahqwas danced in a larger Circle. Pussough was drumming away and singing loudly. He looked like he might even be enjoying himself.

Then came the third *Round* of the song. Matahqwas danced round and round, in an even larger Circle.

By the start of the fourth *Round*, the Rabbit danced in such a large Circle, Pussough could hardly see him.

The big Cat stopped drumming, and yelled out, "Matahqwas! The song is over! It is time to eat you, now!"

The Rabbit yelled back, "What!?"

"I said the song is over, it is time to eat you, now!"

Matahqwas hollered, "Pussough, forgive me but I must call your attention to your mistake! That was only three *Rounds*!"

The Cat thought to himself for moment and scratched his whiskers. He was sure that was four. And it was. But Pussough was very hungry and didn't want to waste time in dispute.

"One more *Round*, it is, Matahqwas!" He shouted.

As he sang this *extra Round*, Matahqwas danced in a Circle so large, Pussough could no longer see him.

"Where are you, Matahqwas?" Pussough bitterly roared. "It is time for me to claim my feast!"

Matahqwas was long gone. He danced away, off and back on the Path to the Melting Moon Gathering.

—⚍—

Clouds of Mosquitoes began to gather around Bear and Crow. Bear swatted and Crow fanned his wings, as the Insects tried to bite.

"You troublesome creatures, go away!" Bear demanded.

Crow swiped, pecked at them, but they kept coming.

"I cannot," Crow complained, "Share a Story like this!"

Nearby, Assounch, or Skunk, was searching for food.

He overheard the commotion. He walked over and decided to lend Crow and Bear some help.

He pounded the ground twice with his front paws, then pointed his backside toward the swarm of Mosquitos. He then put to use his greatest weapon. All the flying insects quickly dispersed.

Crow said, "Taubotne, Assounch." (Thank you, Skunk.)

Skunk replied, "I am on the hunt for food. But I would not mind a respite to listen to a Story from you, Crow."

Bear asked, "Skunk, are you sure?" As he covered his nose with his paw. "Perhaps you should keep going?" He suggested.

Skunk sat down, took out his pipe and lit it.

He took a puff and replied, "Nonsense, Bear. Surely, I have time to hear one."

Crow said, "Yes. I recall a Story I think you should pay attention to."

The Story of Matchemungqus

A long time ago, it was this way. There was this young, loving Couple of Human Beings from Nipmuc Land.

It was not long before the Woman got pregnant. She gave birth to a beautiful Baby Boy. When the Child was about six months old, the family went out on an ice-fishing trip. The Mother wrapped the little One in soft Deer skin and strapped him to her back. Father, Mother, and Baby set off to ice fish in a place known today as '*Muschopauge Pond*' in Rutland, Massachusetts.

They were making a good catch and having good time. On the North side of the Lake, the Forest was thick with tall Trees. Pines, Oaks, and White Birch stretched all the way into Wachusett Mountain, and beyond. Not far from the family, there was something watching them. It was concealed amongst the large Trees and brush. It peered out from an opening between the dense Pines.

The Couple was unaware that they were being watched. They continued to fish and chuckle. The Sky darkened as a Winter Storm was quickly moving in.

The Nipmuc Man looked up at the thick clouds, as heavy snow began to fall. He told his Wife that they need to get going, and fast.

They packed up their fish and supplies and headed off the ice. They took a few steps onto shore and fell into a hole. The hole was about 3 feet deep and 5 feet wide. They climbed out and soon realized that it was not a hole. It was a giant footprint. The footprint belonged to what was watching them. A Stone-Monster Giant.

They panicked and looked around for the creature. Snow was falling, rapidly. White, puffy flakes were whipping and swirling around with the gusting wind. They heard a loud shrieking growl coming from the Trees. The Baby began to cry. The ground below their feet rumbled. The creature parted through two giant Pine Trees and charged through them. The Human Beings darted away towards a narrow trail, hoping the tight path would slow the beast down. They ran as fast as their legs would go.

It has been said, that these Stone-Monster Giants live somewhere behind the large Mountains to the North. They would come down, from time to time, and feed. They feed on Human Being flesh. And their favorite part of the Human Beings, are the bones. And this monster was very hungry. The Stone-Monster Giant tore after the Human Beings, shaking the Earth with each big step.

The snow continued to heap and pile, rapidly. Ice glazed over the family's eyebrows, as the cold, wind-driven snow was blinding their vision. The Couple trudged forward. Their moccasins sank deeper, and deeper, in the snow with each step.

The Stone-Monster Giant was gaining on them, as it crashed through large Trees and let off a hideous growl that boomed through the valley. The Man grabbed his Wife's hand to help quicken her pace. She slipped and fell, face first, into the snow. He snatched her up to her feet, while still moving forward. The Mother wiped snow from her cheeks and the Child. She quickly passed the Baby to her Husband. This helped them move a little faster. But the beast was still coming.

They realized they were not going to outrun this formidable creature. They looked for a place to hide. The Storm was raging and the monster was chasing. The Child's cry made the couple more fearful and desperate. They frantically searched for a place to conceal and shelter themselves. Everything was getting buried under the snow and ice.

Finally, they saw a felled Elm Tree. It was covered with snow but there was a hole on the side. The opening was only large enough for the Baby to fit inside. There was nowhere for the Parents to hide. They decided that they could at least save the Baby. The Parents cried and said their goodbyes to the Infant. They tucked him gently, and deep, inside the hole. They yelled and ran away to distract the monster, to get him away from the Baby.

In a short time, the Stone-Monster Giant caught both of them. The beast began to feed. Once the monster filled its belly with the Couple, it headed back toward the Mountains.

The Elm Tree was soon completely covered in snow. But it was nice, warm, and dry inside. And that was not all, for the Baby Boy was not alone. There was another family already living in there, a family of *Assounch* (Skunk). The Mother Skunk had recently given birth to three Babies. The Human Being Child was thrown in among them.

Instead of killing the Baby, the Mother and Father Skunk took pity on him. They disliked the Stone-Monster Giants, too. The Mother nudged the Human Being Baby closer to her three, to get more warmth.

The Skunk family treated the Baby as one of their own. They taught him how to survive and hunt; and most importantly, how to protect himself. The Assounch have a special power to defend themselves: a horrible, nose-curling liquid-stench, that they can propel at a great distance.

But this Human Being didn't have that. The Skunk family needed to help him find a way to guard himself or he would, surely, die. A very old, wise, and powerful *Skunk Healer* was sent to see what he could do for the Boy. He prepared a mix of herbs and roots. Then, he added a special *leafy Plant* that grows near Swamps. This *leafy Plant* is said to be so potent and enchanting, that it can grow right through the Winter snow and melt it. The *Skunk Healer* said a prayer to bless the Medicine. He then fed the elixir to the Boy.

In a very short time, the Boy was able to produce his own stinky repellent which would rival any Skunk. Now, the little Boy was able to defend himself against any foe who would dare approach. He would stomp his little feet, bend over and aim. The horrible odor would shoot in the air, causing his enemies to flee.

The Skunks were all very pleased and nodded their heads in approval.

And this, we are told, is how the Very First, Human Beings, ever had a stench—or as we sometimes call it: *Farts*.

By the time the Boy was 12 years old, the Skunk People felt it was time the Boy return to live amongst the Two Legged. The Boy parted ways with his Skunk relatives and wandered into a Nipmuc village. Nobody had known where the Boy had come from, when he rejoined the Tribe. However, he did look well fed and the people accepted him into the Clan. He was adopted by an elderly couple and moved into their *Wetu*.

The Nipmuc people quickly realized there was something different about this Boy. He stunk. They had never smelled anything so terrible, like that coming from a Human Being. No Two Legged had had farts before and it was just as shocking to hear, as it was as horrible to smell. People's faces would pucker, their eyes would water, they'd cough and sometimes choke or get sick, due to the foul stench. He was named, *'Matchemungqus:'* He Who Smells Bad.

In the beginning people tried to help. They scrubbed his body over, and over, to see if they could wash off the stink. It did not work. They also tried changing what he ate, but that didn't take away the horrid smell. Matchemungqus also tried as hard as he could to stop the smell from coming from him. But the harder he tried, the more nervous he became. And with that, even more farts came.

The other children refused to play any games with him. Matchemungqus was constantly being teased. They threw sticks and dirt balls at him while they called him all kinds of vulgar names. Nobody wanted Matchemungqus around.

His parents moved to the very edge of the village and kept Matchemungqus inside, for his own protection. And when that happened, the air was fresh, again.

Life for the Tribal folks resumed as normal. Normal for everyone, except Matchemungqus. He spent all his days on the far side of the village, unseen, inside the *Wetu*. Matchemungqus was very sad and lonely.

A few months went by and it was a warm Spring day. Some Clan Mothers were sitting in front of the *Longhouse*. They had just finished cooking some stew in a large pot. The Ladies were chatting among themselves as the delicious meal was cooling over the low embers.

Suddenly, the stew rippled violently across the vessel. Their conversation came to an abrupt halt. They could hear a low thump coming from the distance and echoing throughout valley. With each thump, the soup stirred some more. Thump. Thump. Thump! They anxiously turned to one another, for they knew what this had to be.

Dozens of vicious Stone-Monster Giants were on the move. They were storming down the Mountains at a rapid pace. They were heading straight towards the Nipmuc village. Their bulky and gigantic legs crashed forward. Their arms were like giant rock hammers with razor-jagged claws on the end; knocking and cutting down everything in their path.

Their heads were huge boulders with eyes of red glowing Stone. They had very large, chomping jaws. These monster's teeth were made of long Stone spikes, sharpened, to a point. And in the middle of their faces, were their enormous noses, that resembled a beak of a Bird. It was the only part of them not made of Stone. It was brown and made of something like a soft, fleshy Tree bark. They had an acute sense of smell, which helped them sniff out Hunan Beings hiding in small places.

The Woman yelled out to all the people of the village, "Run, run and hide! The Stone-Monster Giants are coming!"

Everybody stopped what they were doing and started running in every direction. But it was too late. The creatures were already scattered around the village. The Stone creatures belched out hideous roars and moans as they gave chase to the Human Beings. The beasts began to snatch the terrified people up, at will. Grabbing them however they could: by the hair, legs, arms; any part they could clutch in their massive and rough, rock hands. The Nipmucs rallied their best Warriors to try and stop the attack. They shot hundreds of arrows at the creatures. The arrows just bounced off. It seemed to only make them angrier. The Stone-Monster Giants were stuffing their mouths with people, using both hands.

They chomped rapidly, as slivers of bone were shooting out their mouths, with each bite. People were crying, kicking, and screaming as the monsters were chewing their way through the entire Tribe.

Matchemungqus and his family's Wetu sat on the remote side of the village. The monsters had not made it there, yet. But they could view the horror from their lodge. The old Man told Matchemungqus and his wife, "There is nothing we can do for them. But we have a chance to escape if we run, now!"

Matchemungqus looked on, sadly, at the people, and said, "No! I won't run, I am going to fight them!"

The old Man tried to stop him, but Matchemungqus charged toward the Stone-Monster Giants.

He ran up to a rock beast that was devouring a Man, "Stop it!" He shouted, "Stop it, now! All of you, get out of here!"

The creature laughed so hard, that pieces of the Man came falling out of its mouth.

Another monster was drooling, smacking its rock lips, and then began charging towards Matchemungqus.

As the Stone-Monster Giant got close, Matchemungqus stomped his feet and shouted, *"Noowadchanumun Ne Moskehtu Wutche Assounch!"*

Those words stopped the creature with a jarring fright. An icy chill went shooting up his stony spine and the beast started trembling.

There was only one thing Stone-Monster Giants feared. One thing they dare never cross paths with.

"Noowadchanumun Ne Moskehtu Wutche Assounch!" The Boy shouted, once more. These ominous words translate to: "I am protected by the power of the mighty Skunk!"

That stormy Winter afternoon, many years ago, when Matchemungqus was placed in that Elm log; the monsters did smell his flesh. But they also caught the scent of the one Animal that is the terror of all their nightmares. They dare not go anywhere near the Skunk's home. Assounch Medicine saved Matchemungqus when he was just a Baby. Now, he would use that same gift that was shared with him, to save his people.

Matchemungqus stomped his feet, aimed and let loose a heavy waft of his odor. He delivered the most putrid smell you could ever imagine. The entire body of the monster that confronted Matchemungqus began to convulse and rattle. His huge, beak-like nose began to split open in tiny cracks. The small cracks quickly grew larger. Then his nose just crumbled right off of his face.

His head exploded into tiny pebbles, letting loose a shower of small Stones that went sailing through the Sky. The rest of his body collapsed into a pile of rubble. Matchemungqus went after the other monsters and sprayed more of his *Skunk Medicine*. Five more creatures came to a stone crushing end. The Stone-Monster Giants went into a great panic and ran. Some running so fast, that they accidentally trampled over other monsters that were ahead of them. A few more were destroyed just by the creatures crashing into each other while trying to escape.

Matchemungqus was young and swift. He was catching every one of them. The Stone-Monster Giants ran for the Mountains. They ran toward the valley, Rivers, and some even towards the Ocean. But none of them could outrun the smell. When the scent hit their tender noses, their bodies smashed to bits. Stones of various sizes and shapes, tumbled and scattered all throughout the land and waters. Matchemungqus had saved the village.

All the Nipmuc people came out and celebrated. They thanked Matchemungqus over, and over, and apologized for pushing him away. They gifted him with a rope of Wampum and a string of Eels to feast on. Matchemungqus thanked them, and said, "I am so happy to help. I know my smell is too strong for you, so I will go back and live with the Assounch. They are my family, too."

One of the Men said, "Do not leave us. What if the creatures return? What will we do? We need you, here."

Matchemungqus thought for a moment. "I have a plan," he said. He left the village and went to visit the powerful and wise *Skunk Healer*. He returned the next day to the Nipmuc village. He brought back some of the same Medicine he was given, as a Baby. He gave all of them a small amount of the Skunk mix. Some ended up getting a little bit more than others. But now, all had a little bit of the power within them.

They all knew the smell could be very offensive to each other. The people agreed that they would be very careful with their smell. They said if they felt the need to release some odor, they would step outside their Wetu, because the smell was only for destroying the Stone-Monster Giants. Even today, you can still see the heads, legs, and arms of what remains of the Stone-Monster Giants of long ago, scattered throughout Nipmuc Land.

—ɯ—

Skunk tapped his pipe on a log, emptied out the ash, and said, "Ah, a marvelous Story, indeed, Brother Crow. I truly enjoyed it. May all the Stories return to you and may the power of Assounch protect all Storytellers. Now, I must go."

Crow nodded in appreciation. Bear smiled at Skunks departure.

Crow was feeling much better.

"Bear, I have many stories coming to my Heart."

"As you should, Crow," Bear said, "You always did enjoy the telling of Stories—and talking."

"Yes, I do." Crow said with vigor, "I have much more to tell."

Wild Cat Learns a Lesson

It was this way, long ago. At a time when Mother Earth was covered in much snow, there was a very large *Pussough* (Wildcat), who you should know about.

Back then, Wildcats were much larger and had long beautiful tails. Like then, as now, they were superb hunters, especially, in the dark of night. Pussough would stealthily approach his prey, quickly grasp hold with his very sharp claws, and then eat them up.

This Pussough was one of the best hunters of his Clan. He also seemed to never get enough food. Even when he was full, he would still eat more, and more.

He crept through the snow, eating this and eating that; devouring every Animal that he could track down. As he continued to stuff himself, his belly stretched way out.

And the more he ate, the larger Pussough grew. He just got bigger, and bigger. He became the largest Wild Cat, ever. Pussough then began chasing the other Wild Cats away and stealing their food. When the other Wildcats would ask him to share, he would hiss loudly, and shout, "Mine! All for me to eat and nobody else!"

But then, he grew so enormous, he became too slow to hunt, and too heavy to climb. His stomach was so large that it dragged across the snow. He now had a hard time moving around. He became desperate and angry. He was hungry and needed to figure out a new way to get food.

He captured a sleeping Squirrel. Pussough shook him until he awoke.

Pussough then forced him to hold up his stomach, while he walked, searching for more food. This giant Wildcat threatened to eat him, in one bite, if he refused to comply. The poor, little Squirrel was very afraid and did as he was commanded.

Pussough was huge and it was not easy for the scanty Squirrel to carry out the task. He had to burrow under the snow, just to get underneath the Wildcat's fat belly. With a face full of snow, and very cold; Squirrel pushed up on the massive stomach, and just barely got it up and out of the snow. So, the Squirrel's body was under the snow, while his little hands pushed up the Wildcats belly. Off Pussough went, looking for prey.

Squirrel worked hard holding up the massive stomach as Pussough looked all around, up and down, searching for food. But even with Squirrels help, the extra-large Wildcat was too slow to catch anything. Then, they wandered around the Forest, looking for someone else's food to take.

Pussough noticed some peculiar tracks in the snow. He had never seen them before. But he figured wherever they lead, there will probably be food.

"Push on!" He shouted to Squirrel. And the two of them followed the tracks. The trail lead to a lodge. It was the winter lodge of *Hobomook*.

Hobomook is known to our Nipmuc people, as a Trickster, with mystic powers. Many times, causing mischief or chaos with his influence and Magic. Other times, he may help by giving you a warning, or teaching a lesson. Since we never know what to expect, it is always wise to stay clear of Hobomook. The giant Wildcat sniffed his way to the Hobomook den. The weary, little Squirrel was struggling and shivering, but still holding up Pussough's belly.

Pussough used his huge claws and scratched his way in. He looked in and saw the home was crammed with food. His mouth watered and he smacked his lips. Squirrel sensed danger by being in the lodge. He warned the big Wildcat that they should leave. Pussough ignored the warning and told Squirrel to stop talking.

He swiped at him and grabbed him by his tail. He then tied up Squirrel to the top of the Wigwam, by his tail. Pussough said, "There, you can stay up there while I eat. You better hope I am full or you will be next." The wet and trembling Squirrel hung there by his tail, swaying back and forth, in terror.

Pussough began to feast on all of Hobomook's Winter goods. Dried meats, fish, Berries, Corn, beans; anything and everything he could find to graze on. As the humungous Animal gorged himself, he carelessly knocked over Hobomook's bed, destroyed his pots, baskets, and other supplies while searching for more food.

By this time, Hobomook was returning home after being out on a hunt. He got near the entrance of his lodge and stopped short. He noticed his lodge door was open. He slowly pulled out his hunting knife. The handle was carved from a portion of the spine of a Stone-Monster Giant. The long blade was made of black Quartz, that was once buried deep in place called, *Keekomowadachaug*, which means: The Place Where the Earth Trembles.

Hobomook crouched, tilted his head from side to side, as he looked into his home. He could hear the banging around of his things and loud chomping. He grumbled under his breath and his eyes tightened with anger. Hobomook released a menacing grin. Then, he leapt high in the air. He landed just inside his lodge entrance. He looked in just in time to see Pussough finishing off the last of his goods.

Hobomook was furious. "How dare you enter my home!" He shouted. The giant Wildcat's hair stood up on its back. He held up his paw with his claws out, and hissed at the Sorcerer. Hobomook sharply glared back, pointing his knife toward him.

"Do you not know who I am?" The Trickster asked. "I am the great Sorcerer Hobomook! This blade is not just for cutting. I can do many things with this knife," he warned. "Yes, you are a giant Wildcat, but I can easily turn you into a Mosquito!"

Pussough gasped. He quickly dropped his paw, tucked his long soft tail between his legs, and bowed his head low. "Forgive me, great Hobomook, do not hurt me. My problem is that I am too large and too slow to catch anything, so I have to eat what I can."

Hobomook began to think. He asked, "You are too slow? And, is it also that you have been too greedy, taking more than you need?"

"Yes, I have. I have taken much more than I need," Pussough replied. "Please do not turn me into a Mosquito," he pleaded.

Hobomook looked at him sharply, "You stole my food. You destroyed my lodge; but I can forgive you, if you promise never to come here, again."

"Yes, yes!" Pussough happily agreed, "I will not come back!"

"But because you stole from me," Hobomook explained, "You are going to have to give me something, in return."

The Wildcat looked up at the Squirrel and said, "Hobomook, you can take him, take this Squirrel."

Hobomook looked him over and said, "No, I do not want him. I want your tail. You have such a long, beautiful tail. I like it very well."

The Wildcat didn't want to give up his tail, but he had no choice. Hobomook grabbed Pussough by the tail and used his special knife to cut it off. Hobomook took the tail and put it on himself. He then began laughing and danced around the lodge, swinging his new tail, back and forth.

Hobomook shouted, and pointed to the Wildcat, "Now, get out and do not ever come back, or next time you will lose more than a tail!"

The Wildcat ran out as fast as his huge body would let him.

And that is why Pussough has a short tail, to this day. Squirrel, who was still hanging from the top of the lodge asked, "What about me?"

Hobomook stopped dancing for a moment, scratched his chin, "Yes, what about *you*? You were the Wildcat's aid. Another thief! How should I destroy you?"

"Oh, no!" Cried Squirrel, "I had nothing to do with it, I was forced here!"

Hobomook replied, "Since you say this was not of your doing, how can you prove to me you won't be greedy and steal more food?"

"I have a way," said Squirrel. "From now on, when I gather food, I will only eat a small amount. I will save the rest for hard times when there is not enough to eat."

Hobomook said, "What a wonderful idea. I shall let you live."

Hobomook intensely gazed at the little Squirrel as his body swayed back and forth, through the air.

Hobomook said, "And because I believe you to be honest, I, the great Hobomook, will give you a special gift."

Hobomook loosened the Squirrel. He laid him down on his back and looked at the Squirrel's tired little arms. He slowly and gently touched his black Quartz knife blade along the side of the Squirrel's arms and the skin began to stretch out, shaping them into furry wings.

"There," said Hobomook, "this will help you get away from that Wildcat the next time he tries to torment you. Now, you will fly away from him, like a bird."

This is why, today, we have Flying Squirrel. Those who are greedy and are not helpful, always end and up with less. But those who are honest and share, always end up with more.

—m—

Gift of the Strawberry

Long ago, it was this way. There was a little Girl and her slightly, younger Brother.

They were always quarreling with one another. It seemed that they could never get along. Everywhere they went, there was an argument. One day, they had been squabbling even more than usual. Finally, the little Girl got tired of fighting and ran off into the woods. She ran and ran, deeper into the woods. After she grew weary of running, she began walking. She walked for a long time.

The sun was shining pleasantly that warm day. Birds were singing happily in the Trees and there were some Squirrels gathering chestnuts under the hot Sky. Soon the Girl forgot all about the disagreement with her Brother. She even laughed to herself thinking how much they needlessly argue. But now, she was lost, thirsty, and hungry. She looked around for something to eat, but couldn't find anything.

The young Girl searched for a Lake or a stream to quench her thirst. But she could not find any Water.

The Sun was beginning to set. The Girl's little Brother, who was back at the village, was deeply worried wondering where could she be. He had set out to search for her. He walked and shouted out her name over, and over. But he could not find her. After walking a great distance, he, too, became thirsty and hungry.

His legs, not being as strong as his big Sister's, could no longer go. So, he laid down to rest.

Weariness and hunger were already taking its toll on the Girl. She also became too weak to go any further and she laid down to rest. She was starting to fall asleep, from sheer exhaustion. Just as her eyes were about to close, something bright from a small bush, caught her attention. It was a bright, red Berry that sparkled like a Crystal. The Berry was shaped like a Heart. This was the first Strawberry ever seen.

The Girl used what little strength left to crawl over to the plant. She picked a Strawberry and examined it. She had never seen anything like this before. But since she was starving and thirsty, she decided to take her chances and eat it.

Tasting one, she found it to be deliciously sweet and thirst quenching. She ate a few more. Soon, she was feeling much better and regaining her strength. But, she was still lost. The Girl missed her little Brother and wished they were together.

She prayed, and prayed, to be with her Brother again.

A glimmering trail of Strawberries appeared on the ground. She followed it, picking one by one. The Berries led her to her Brother. The Boy was weak and lying down under a Tree. The Girl quickly shared some of the sweet, heart-shaped fruit with her Brother.

She told him how regretful she was for arguing with him. Her little Brother quickly regained his strength. He then, also apologized. They embraced each other as the loving Brother and Sister they are now becoming. Then by working *TOGETHER*, they were able to find their way home.

The siblings brought back the first Strawberries to all the people in the village. They explained that these were the *'fruit of forgiveness.'* And maybe that's why they are shaped like a Heart. From that day on, the Brother and Sister got along, quite well. For the Strawberry had brought them together. Strawberries have come to be known as a symbol of forgiveness, friendship, and Love. From that, came the Strawberry Moon Ceremony.

Each year when the Strawberry Moon Ceremony is held, it is customary for anyone holding a grudge against someone to invite that person to the gathering. There, they will offer the person a Strawberry, as a symbol of forgiveness and Love.

—⁓—

The Three Sisters

Long ago there were Three Sisters. Each one very beautiful. But the young girls were very different from each other.

One was very tall, slender and had long yellow smooth hair.

The other Sister was a little shorter. She had long, curly and shiny brown hair.

The third Sister was shorter than the other two. Her hair was radiant black, wavy, but was also very long.

These Sisters loved each other very much.

But even though they loved each other dearly, these differences brought about arguments among them all the time.

The endless bickering lead them to not spend any time together.

Each Sister kept to herself, unless it was to disagree with the other.

Their Mother saw this and was upset.

She urged them to get along and share with one another. The girls refused.

So the Mother thought for a long time, what could she do?

A few days had passed. The Three Sisters were out in the garden.

They were arguing amongst themselves, as always.

They were going at it pretty good; shouting, pointing and shaking their hands in the air.

The Mother asked them to stop the bickering at once.

She asked the Three Sisters to sit down in the garden beside each other.

But the girls were very stubborn. Just as one Sister would sit down, the other would get up and leave. Then when the other would come back and sit, the other Sister would walk away. Back and forth they went, not wanting to sit together. Not wanting to sit as one.

The Mother grew very tired of this. Finally, she got them all to sit in the garden.

The Mother said, "I want you girls to listen. You Three Sisters are all very special and unique. But you are also a part of me. Each of you. You need to see the beauty not only in yourself but each other."

The girls frowned, mumbled, cut their eyes at each other as they fidgeted about.

The Mother said, "I want you to sit here until you make peace. Sit here until you resolve your differences."

Then the Mother took each girls hair and held it in her hands. She gently brought all the girl's hair together. The yellow, brown and black hair was twisted into one long beautiful braid.

She told them, "Stay here until you all have resolved this quarrel. Once you have come to an accord, unloose the braid. When I see, you have undone the braid, I will know you have made peace."

The girls sat for a long, long time. The Mother returned often to check on them. She noticed the braid had not been undone. As the girls sat in the garden, the long braid began to take root in the garden.

When the Mother returned this time, Corn, Beans and Squash grew in the spot where her daughters sat.

The Mother was sad that her daughters were gone.

But then, the plants spoke to the Mother and said. "Do not despair Mother. We have come together in a way that honors our differences as you had asked of us. And we will always be with you. And what we have, we will share with many generations to come. We shall teach that even with great differences among us; we can come together and share with each other. And when we share with one another, a new strength is born."

Sister Corn provided a structure for her Sister Beans to climb, eliminating the need for poles. Sister Beans provided nutrients to Mother Earth that helped her Sisters grow healthy and strong. Sister Squash spread out along the ground, blocking the sunlight, to prevent the weeds from growing on her Sisters. Sister Squash also grew wide leaves to keep moisture in the soil, and grew prickly hairs on her vine to deter pests.

The Three Sisters teach us: that by sharing with one another we not only can heal from within, but also become stronger in Unity.

—✺—

Tears of the Cedar Tree: A Love Story

Long ago, it was this way. There was a very, valiant Nipmuc Warrior.

He was very handsome and the best hunter in the village. The Man took great pride in his prowess with his bow and fighting skills. But his greatest joy in life, was his Wife, who he loved, dearly. Every successful hunt and battle, was all to impress and provide for her.

One day, to his sad surprise, she left him for another. The warrior was overwhelmed with sadness. He did not understand the reason for her sudden departure. He went to her and asked what went wrong. She told him, "You are a very good Man. You are brave and, oh, so handsome but yet, I have fallen in Love with another."

The Man was feeling rather low-spirited and begged her to stay. She declined. Being the kind of Man he was, he was not going to give up on the Love of his life, easily. He went to her lodge and sang her songs. He even learned to play the flute just to amaze her and sang beautiful tunes.

She continued to reject him. He then went on the hunt, like never before. He caught many large Animals, then gifted the meat and hides to her and all of her relatives. She was thankful, but still refused him and his Love.

She simply told him, "I am sorry. As I have said, I am now in Love with another." The Nipmuc Warrior went on, for more than 13 Moons, to try and win back her affection. And still, she did not take him back. He was exhausted and heartbroken. His heart would not allow him to live without her. He did not hunt. He did not take part in anymore battles. He felt hopeless without her. He did not know what else to do.

He decided to go on a voyage. He travelled to the village of his people's most despised enemies. When he arrived at the rival Nation, there were dozens of fierce fighters doing a *War Dance*, preparing for a battle. The Nipmuc Man was unarmed as he approached their village.

He walked right into the center of their *War Dance*. Several of the men were dancing and shouting out their victories in battle, then bashing an axe, in a wooden pole, at the center of the Circle. The Nipmuc shouted to them, "You, men! I am right here!"

All the Warriors suddenly halted. Their eyes cut, angrily, into him. They studied him up and down. Some Warriors moving in close and others stepping further away. They began to whisper among themselves.

The lead Warrior stepped forward, and said, "We know you. Talk of your troubles has travelled further than the *Twin Rivers*. You were once a great Warrior. But now, you spend your days in much sorrow."

"Do not speak, just fight!" The Nipmuc shouted, "All of you, fight me, now!"

The rival Warrior said, "No, we can see you are a Man with a bothered mind, and a broken Heart. Your sadness and suffering has now entered our Circle. It is bad luck to kill a Man with a broken Heart. We will not fight you, today. Leave now, and take your sadness with you. Go!" They demanded.

Three of the men took hold of him and carried him to the edge of the village. They tossed him down, near some bushes. The Nipmuc Man got up from the ground, yelled some insults, and headed for the thick Forest. He walked past a splendid field of Wildflowers. They filled the air with sweet fragrances. There were also tall grasses. Dragonflies and Humming Birds danced above them. He walked by all sorts of wild Berries, as he neared a dense area of red Maple and Oak Trees. He strode for a very, long time through a sea of tall, white Pine Trees, that stretched high in the Sky. Soon he was in a section of Willow Trees that hugged along a bubbling stream. The thick and green leaves made a canopy along the edges of the Water.

He walked, and walked some more. All the while, he was thinking of his lost Love. After journeying a bit further, he reached his destination: The Sacred Cedar Forest, the place of Medicine, Magic, and mystery. As he entered, there was a thick mist in the air. It was dark for the Cedar Trees were tall and blocked out the Sky.

He chose this, as the place where he would die. He dropped to his knees, onto to the bumpy ground, were roots ran in every direction. He then lay face down on the ground, that was unusually dry, as it had not rained in over two weeks. His long hair rested wildly on the Earth. The Man wept.

He cried all day and into the night. Come the morning, he was still flowing out tears of sadness. He wept for several more days. Large pools of tears were filling the ground all around him. The soil that was parched was now drenched in the tears of this sad Warrior.

The Cedar Trees all around him began to drink it up. They were being well nourished by the Man's tears, all throughout the Cedar grove. Some of the branches that were browning from the drought, started turning bright green.

The Man was near death. He was dying from a broken Heart. Suddenly, the ground began to shake beneath his weeping body.

There was a large Cedar Tree to the left of him, and another one just to his right. Both of the Trees began to move their branches. Each Tree stretched out a branch toward the Man. They reached under his arms. They began to slowly lift him. His body was very heavy. Not from his weight, but from his sadness. The Cedar Trees strained a little, but they continued on. Soon his body was rising. They pulled his sagging and weak body to his feet.

Paponetin (West Wind) Came blowing in with mighty force. It pushed him a little forward. The strong gust blew his hair, uncontrollably. Paponetin blew in-between the strands of his hair, then sectioned and twisted it into one long braid, that rested down the center of his back. Then a thin, Cedar branch whipped around the bottom end of the hair, to tie it off.

One Cedar Tree began to speak:

"Your pain has given us life; your pain has nourished our roots. And it is so, that out of pain, that there will be growth, my Son. Out of this pain, there will be a new journey for you. You have been blessed by the Great Spirit with many gifts. Continue to share what you have been asked to share. Make good use of your blessings. Be sad, no more. When your pain is too heavy, come back and we will lift you with these words of truth, once more. If you are too far away, lean on your family, of which, you have many. And that, my Son, is a wonderful gift to have.

And you have one other gift," continued the Sacred Tree, "The gift of giving Love. And in time, someone will come that will need it, desire it, and cherish it forever. Now, go, my son, and live."

The Nipmuc Man felt a new strength come over him. He had much gratitude for his gifts and smiled for the first time in many Moons. He walked back to his village and, once again, shared his many gifts with his Tribe. They say, it was not long before, he found a new Love. This time, the Love was much stronger than the first Love. They say, he lived to be very old and had many children and grandchildren. And so, everything happens for a reason.

Even today, when you are in the Sacred Cedar Forest, be still and listen. For sometimes you can hear the Trees cry and release the sadness and sorrow of the broken-hearted Nipmuc Man's tears that went so deep into their roots, so long ago.

—⚭—

"Caw! – Wake up, Bear, wake up! Did you not hear the Stories?" asked Crow. "I spoke of many things."

Bear was curled up next to an Oak Tree. He began to slowly stretch, then stood up and yawned. "Crow, I did hear the Stories. I listened with my Heart, while I checked the inside of my eyes."

Crow turned his head said to side in disbelief.

"Pussough will never tangle with Hobomook, again. I am sure of it. Ah yes, the Strawberry, indeed, the symbol of Love and forgiveness. And, one of my favorite treats. It goes splendid with Corn, Beans and Squash. Most certainly, the Three Sisters show us a powerful unity of life! And, Speaking of Love, The Tears of Cedar Tree is a very good Tale, Netomp."

"I see, Bear; your ears are wide open, even though your eyes are closed."

"Surely, Crow," Bear replied, "Many Two Legged and Four Legged, for that matter, have wandered into my lodge during my Winter slumber. They think I am in such a deep sleep that I do not notice them. Yes, I sleep, and I sleep well. But my ears are always awake."

Bear looked at Crow, thoroughly, and acknowledged, "Crow, you look much better. I think you will find your Dream, soon."

"Bear, wait, listen to me. I have another Story."

Mukkiah Weesug

For those of you who have never heard of the *Mukkiah Weesug*, sometimes called *'Little People,'* there are many Stories of them from various Tribes of the East. This is one such story:

Long ago, it was this way. A Nipmuc hunter set off deep in the woods to search for food for his family.

He searched for days but did not have any luck. After growing tired, he stopped to build a small lodge and fire. Before he went to sleep, he prayed for better luck on the next day. Early the next morning, he was abruptly awakened by some strange sounds. The noise was coming from some brush nearby. He slowly turned on his side to reach for his bow. He eased himself up. The Man quietly walked, in the direction of the sound, with an arrow pulled back on his bow. He took aim in the direction of the shaking shrub. A tiny creature jumped out.

The Man was stunned and did not shoot.

"What are you?!" He asked.

The Creature answered, "I am the Guardian of this Forest. The Protector and Great Warrior of the Swamps and Tree Spirits. I keep the balance in this place."

The Man laughed and said, "But you are no larger than frog, and just as ugly."

Mukkiah Weesug, frowned and replied, "You are a fool, and a bad hunter. I can show you how to catch all you will ever need. However, you must give me that string of *Wampum* that's around your neck."

"I see, you want my *Wampum*? I earned this in battle, ugly Little One." The Man sharply replied, "I am not going to just hand it over to *you*."

"Then starve, you foolish Human Being!" Warned Mukkiah Weesug.

The Nipmuc Man went back to hunt. Another day passed without a catch. It was as if all the animals had vanished from the countryside. Finally, the Warrior gave in. He went back to the Little One, and said, "Here, here is my *Wampum*."

Mukkiah Weesug ran up his leg, jumped on his forearm, and snatched the string of *Wampum* out of his hand. He leaped down and ran across the Forest floor as the string of *Wampum* dragged behind him. He yelled, "Follow me!"

The Man could barely keep up with him. For a tiny creature, he was very swift.

They travelled a great distance, crossing several Paths. At one point, the Man had to struggle to jump over a large, felled Tree, along the trail. Mukkiah Weesug simply went under it, without missing a step. Finally, they came to a hole in the ground.

The Little Being jumped in the hole and disappeared beneath the Earth.

The Man stood above the hole for a moment, trying to look down into its darkness. He strained his eyes, but could not see anything.

He said, "You! Down there, Little Ugly One, where should I hunt?"

After a few moments, he came back up. He pointed and instructed, "Over that way. Cross that stream, and travel South for a short distance, down that trail of crooked Trees." He then jumped back in the hole.

The Man travelled to where he was told. He found the trail, as described. He noticed many, odd-shaped Trees that were extremely bent, crooked, and twisted marking the direction.

The end of the trail opened to a large grove. He immediately saw a large Deer. He pulled back his bow and took the Buck down with one shot. He then went over to carve up the meat. The Nipmuc Man made a small sled out of hemlock. He then began dragging the Deer out of the Forest and back toward his village.

That is when another Mukkiah Weesug appeared. "Kwai, Human Being, I am the Guardian of this Forest. The Protector and Great Warrior of the Swamps and Tree Spirits. I keep the balance in this place. Human Being, before you take this Animal, you must leave some behind, as an offering."

The Man scoffed, "I know your kind. I have met another like you. It must be that you are Brothers; for you are just as ugly, if not more, than he."

"No. I am not his Brother. I am his Sister. Listen, Human Being, you must leave something. An offering."

The Man chuckled, "You, Mukkiah Weesug, amuse me. Yet, you are wise. And brave. Very well," the Man said. He left a portion of the meat and some Tobacco by a Tree. He went back to his village. His family ate well and were very pleased with his catch.

Some months passed and another hunter came upon the same Forest. This Man had heard of the Mukkiah Weesug and was prepared to out-smart them. He refused to share and had plans to trick them. As he went searching the Forest for his meal, he saw nothing. And, just as before, the Mukkiah Weesug appeared. He said, "Kwai, Human Being, I am the Guardian of this Forest. The Protector and Great Warrior of the Swamps and Tree Spirits. I keep the balance in this place. If you give me a gift, I will show you the best hunting grounds."

The Man gave him some pink and purple *Wampum*. The Little Being was delighted. The Man followed him to his hole. Mukkiah Weesug came back out and said, "Travel over that hill. You will see a small Lake. Then, follow the trail of the crooked Trees. That is where you will make a superb catch."

The Man began to walk in that direction. Once he was out of sight, he hid behind a large Stone. He waited until the tiny creature fell asleep. He then came back to the hole. He dug deep into the Earth. He discovered the underground village of the Little People. He saw they had many bas-kets filled with all sorts of beautiful Wampum, carved and shiny Stones, fine woven baskets, and other precious goods.

The Man said to himself, 'These little beggars will not have my Wampum. What's more, I shall take all of their goods and keep them for myself.'

The Man quickly gathered up the entire treasure and fled. He then went to the hunting grounds, as told by Mukkiah Weesug. He looked and searched, but found nothing. Not even a chipmunk, turkey or rabbit could be found. Soon, the Man was lost. He became worn out, thirsty, and hungry. He was so tired, he could no longer carry all the goods. He dropped everything and continued to walk through the cold and dark Forest. When he could no longer walk, he lied down, beside a Tree. The Man was completely exhausted and fell into a very, deep sleep.

The Mukkiah Weesug showed up in great numbers. They removed his moccasins. Then they put a tiny piece of a branch between each one of his toes. Next, they put another slightly larger piece of wood next to the other; spreading all his toes out, as far as they could go. After that, the Little People went to his fingers and stretched them all out with sticks, the same way. They stuck branches under his arms pushing them out, away from his body. Several Mukkiah Weesug worked together to carry larger branches and saplings and wedged them between the Man's legs and spread his body very wide. Numerous Little People crawled up into the Man's mouth. They placed tiny splinters of wood between each one of his teeth. Then they went back, got slightly larger twigs, and stuck them between each of his teeth, beside the first ones.

The Man awoke in agonizing pain. And he could not move. Every part of his body was stretched and spread in the most painful, and horrifying position. From a mere glance, you could not tell Man, from branch. Dozens of Mukkiah Weesug gathered around him. They picked him up and carried him off. They rushed him towards the trail of crooked Trees. Near the end of the path, they looked for an open space. They dug a hole. They planted the Man in the ground; right next to all the other crooked Trees.

—ɯ—

Corn Doll Woman

Long ago, in a Tribal village in the Northeast, there was a Great Sachem.

He was a leader of a very large Nation. The Sachem had a beautiful, teenage daughter who was treated like royalty. People of the Nation waited on her, hand and foot. She never had to do any work. The girl spent all of her time inside the Wigwam, doing as she pleased.

One Summer, there was a crisis in the village. There was a drought and so, a shortage of food. People had to work harder, and go on longer hunting parties that were far away from home. Despite all of their efforts, they still could not keep up with the demands of the Tribe. They needed more people to help for the survival of the Village.

That's when some people went to the Sachem, and said, "Great Leader, we need your help. We know your Daughter has never had to do any work but we are shorthanded. We need all the help we can get to save the Nation. Could you ask your Daughter to help with the daily tasks?"

The Leader said, "Of course, I would ask her to help." The Chief went to his Daughter, and said, "My beautiful Girl, there is a great calamity outside of the lodge. We need every, able person to help out and keep our people nourished. We could use your help doing some tasks. Could you please help?"

"I can surely assist, Father," The Daughter replied.

"This is good," said the Chief, "your task shall be to go down to the River and help the other Women gather the Water for cooking."

The Daughter replied, "Yes, I will do, as you ask."

The Girl had never gone to the River before, she never had to because people had always brought her drinks. The Sachems daughter approached the stream, with her watertight Birch bark basket. She looked into the flowing waters. For the first time, she noticed her own reflection. The girl smiled and thought to herself, 'I *am* very beautiful.'

She continued all day long gazing into the Water at her own reflection with great pleasure; sometimes making poses and silly grins. She was so caught up in staring at her own reflection, she forgot what she was supposed to be doing. When nightfall came, the girl returned, but without any water.

The women who were waiting for the Water needed it to make stew, use for drinks, to help with cleaning, and so, they were very upset. They complained to the Sachem. The Leader asked his Daughter what went wrong. The Girl told him of her magnificent discovery of her own reflection. She apologized for not completing her duty, but said she was too busy enjoying the sight of her own beauty.

The Leader scowled and said, "But Daughter, you have an important job to do. The Village is counting on you. This is not the time for you to do such things."

"Forgive me, Father," the Girl pleaded, "I will be sure to get the Water, tomorrow."

The next day, the Sachem's Daughter headed down to the River, once more, to collect the Water. Once she got there, she began looking at herself in the reflection, saying, "I am so lovely, I should be able to look at myself for a little while, it won't hurt anyone."

Before she knew it, the entire day had passed. Again, she came home that evening, without any Water. This time, the people of the village were extremely upset. Many of them came and stood in front of the Chief's lodge to complain and shout. The Sachem did his best to calm everyone down and assured them he would take care of the situation. He was also angry and disappointed by his Daughter's actions.

He went to her and spoke sharply, "My daughter, the people need your help, but twice, you have disappointed them, and me, by not doing your part. This is very wrong. Such behavior will only lead to trouble."

The girl cried, and said, "I am sorry, Father. I did not mean it. I promise that, tomorrow, I will not do that. I will get the Water, without delay."

The next day, she set off early for the River. As she walked toward the stream, she repeated aloud to herself, 'I'm not going to stare in the Water, I'm not going to stare in the Water…' When she reached the shore, she quickly scooped up the Water and began to head back. But, then she stopped. The Girl thought to herself, 'Well, just one quick look at my beautiful face, won't hurt.'

She walked back to the river and looked down, at her reflection. At that same moment, her face vanished. Her face was gone, forever.

This is why when we make the Corn Husk Doll, it is never with a face. Corn Doll Woman teaches us that, *'It's far better to DO Good, than to just try and LOOK Good.'*

—⁂—

Birch Bark Canoe

A long time ago, it was this way. When our people would decide to build a Birch Bark Canoe, they would go to the East side of the Forest and near a hill.

They would seek out a tiny Birch Tree. Then, they would clear out any other shrubs or small Trees near it. They would come back to Water and nurture it; and to make sure no other larger Trees were blocking the Sunlight.

But this small Tree, was not ready to be a Birch Bark Canoe. Therefore, the generation that had chosen that Tree, would pass on the duties of cultivation to the next generation. And so, that next generation would also come to nurture that Tree, and it would continue to get a little larger. Then, they would hand it on to the next generation to continue the cultivation.

It would take seven generations for that Tree to grow large enough to be harvested and made into a Birch Bark Canoe. And that Seventh Generation knew it was time, because the ones from before, had passed on the Story and knowledge for all that has happened with the Tree. When the Birch Tree is harvested, we give thanks to all the generations before us, who worked so hard to take care of this Tree.

We give thanks because, now, our generation can have that Canoe.

Every year, a new Tree is chosen, in this way. And that generation, who chooses the Birch Tree, knows they will never see that Canoe. But they would start the nurturing process for the Seventh Generation to come. So, when that generation is gone, many future generations will benefit from their choice of that Tree.

Our people always give thanks to the Seven Generations who came before us.

We honor, and thank them, for their sacrifice and duty, that made sure then, that we have all that we need, today. We, in turn, have the same responsibility to do this for the next Seven Generations to come.

—⧸⫞⧹—

Toad Woman of the Swamp

Nipmuc Boys and Girls were always warned by their parents to stay away from the Swamps at night.

It was said, that an old Toad Woman would lure kids into the bog and eat them. This Toad Lady was a master at casting spells. She could turn herself into a cute Chipmunk or pretend to be a reed of grass, as to appear harmless. But once she got hold of the child, her true self would appear. That's when she would pull the Girl, or Boy, down to the pit of the Swamp. They would never be seen again.

There was once a young Girl from the village of Wabbaquassett. She lived with her blind *Okummus* (Grandmother). Late one night, the Grandmother was very sick with a fever and coughing. She needed some herbs that grow in the Swamp. The Girl saw how ill her Grandmother was and desperately wanted to help.

The old Lady said, "I am in need of Waterlily tea, my dear Girl. But it is down by the Swamp. It is too dangerous for you to go at night."

"I do not want you to die, Okummus." The girl cried, "If you die, I will be all alone."

The old Lady coughed, and said, "Very well. If you are going to go, I want you to look your finest. Bring me my special *Sweet Grass* basket."

The Girl did as she was asked. Her Grandmother removed the top of the basket.

She told her Granddaughter, "I am going to give you some things that were gifted to me, a long time ago."

She put her frail and wrinkled hand inside the basket and felt around. She pulled out a necklace. It was made of small red shiny Stones. A hole was pierced through each Stone and strung together with sinew.

"This necklace," the old Woman said, "Was a gift from my Great-Grandmother. Put it on."

Her Granddaughter thanked her and put on the necklace.

Okummus reached into the Sweet Grass basket, again, and pulled out a Wampum headband. Wampum starts out as a Quahog shell, then it is carved into fine beads. The Wampum beads were beautifully designed into purple and white flowers, looping around the whole band.

"This was made by my Great-Grandfather." The Grandmother told her, "Put it on."

She thanked her grandmother and put on the Wampum headband.

The old Lady reached into the Sweet Grass basket, once more. She took out a small leather pouch. Inside the pouch was a glob of Pine Tree sap. The sap was hardened on the outside, but liquid and very sticky in the middle. She told the Girl to keep the pouch by her side.

"Okummus, what is this for?" The Girl asked.

"Granddaughter, when you find the Waterlily Plant, I will then need you to break open this sap and pour it over the Plant. This sap will need to be mixed with the Plant. That will make sure it heals me," the Grandmother instructed.

"Yes, Okummus, I will do just as you say," said the Girl.

With Wampum headband, red Stone necklace, and the leather pouch with sap, the Girl set off for the Swamp with only the Moonlight to guide her. She rushed on and was soon far beyond the safety of her village of Wabbaquassett. She began to notice how thick the air was; it felt heavy, and tasted like wet smoke. She knew the Swamp must be near.

The moonlight sprinkled puddles of light here and there. Odd shadows flickered off bushes, large Stones, and Tree limbs that seemed to follow her.

Crickets, chirping bugs, creaking branches, and many unknown sounds created a rambling ensemble. She spotted the Path that lead to the swamp.

Decaying logs lay waste at the edge of the trail. The felled Trees became a haven for Snakes, Spiders, and other creatures of the night. A sense of unease came over the young Girl. But all she could think about, and distract herself with, was her blind and sick Grandmother.

She hurried down the trail which was layered with crumbling russet leaves and small jagged Stones that were hidden underneath that were painful when occasionally stepped on, from time to time. The wrapping, woody vines had a strangling presence. They crept up, and down, and all around both sides of the Path; like long gristly arms ready to grab you, at any moment. The Girl looked back and it seemed that the footpath was closing in, behind her as she walked deeper into the Forest.

There was only one way to go: forward to the swamp. She took a few more steps and noticed the murky bog. Suddenly, all the chirping and buzzing stopped. The Forest went completely silent. She walked toward the swamp. She was full of fright and could hear her own Heartbeat. But she walked forth.

The Girl's nervous legs carried her to the edge of the murky, gloomy Waters. The pond was still, misty, and appeared green from the Moonlight.

Leafless and warped Trees stood scattered about the bog, like eerie shrines to some troubling force. She took a deep breath and thought about her Grandmother, again. She earnestly searched for the Waterlily.

Finally, she saw one. It was at the edge of the North side of the bog, about 25 steps away. The Girl was very excited and hurried towards it. She walked ten quick steps and began to envision her Grandmother getting healthy from the Medicine. The Girl made it ten more paces towards the lifesaving Waterlily and a smile came over her. She now could see her Okummus drinking the healing tea, being strong and happy. The Girl was now just one step away. As she started to reach out to grab the Plant, a large, hideous beast jumped out in front of her. The Girl screamed, but could not move.

The creature must have been seven feet tall. It had long, sharp fangs hanging from its jaw, scaly skin, and legs like a Frog. Instead of fingers at the end of its lanky arms, it had something that resembled large raptor talons. Its hair was thick, wild, and looked like dangling daggers hanging off its head. It gaped at her, drooling and with its large black eyes that reflected off the Moonlight. The thing had a horrible smell, like rotten Swamp. It was the Toad Woman.

The Toad Woman reached out its gangly arms and made a move near the Girl. She collected herself and ran. Jumping through bushes and tripping over Tree roots, but the Girl ran. But still the Toad Woman was gaining on her, and fast. The creature was only a few paces away. The Girl wanted to defend herself, but had no weapon.

The necklace of red Stones gifted to her, from Okummus, was rumbling across her chest with each racing step. In an instant, the Girl clutched it and ripped it off her neck. Then, she threw it at Toad Woman. The rope of beads hit the monster in the face and fell to the ground. The small Stones came loose and scattered about.

Suddenly, all the stones changed into delicious Raspberries. Toad Woman could not resist them. Toad Woman bent down to stuff them into her mouth. She stumbled forward, grabbing Berries with both hands, pressing them to her scaly body, lest they slip away. Eating the fruit slowed Toad Woman down. The Girl was able to get away and hide, while the creature gorged on the Berries. She did not want to go back home without the Waterlily.

After getting lost in the darkness, she was able to find her way back near the Swamp. But Toad Woman also made it back to her murky den. The Girl made a quick dash for the Waterlily. Just as before, the Toad Woman was there to confront her. Toad Woman screeched and attacked. The Nipmuc Girl dashed away through the Woods.

Toad Woman gave chase. As the Girl ran, she could feel the creature's hot breath steaming against her back. She feared Toad Woman would catch her soon.

She snatched loose the Wampum headband gifted to her, from Okummus. The Girl then hurled it at the beast. It struck Toad Woman in the eye and fell to the ground.

The headband was now broken into tiny pieces.

The finely carved Wampum beads, turned back into large Quahog shells.

The creature stepped on them cutting her feet, badly, on the sharp edges. Toad Woman let out a hideous howl, as the shells sliced into her lanky feet. Enraged, it limped after the Girl, blood splattering everywhere. The agile Nipmuc Girl was easily able to outrun the injured creature. She hid nearby and waited for her chance to go back to the Swamp, to retrieve the lifesaving Plant for Okummus.

Meanwhile, Toad Woman licked her wounds and hobbled back to the bog.

She was furious with the Nipmuc Girl. Toad Woman understood what the young gal was after. 'This Girl is swift and full of tricks,' thought the Toad Woman.

"It is better if I use my Magic to catch and eat her," she said.

Toad Woman plunged in the bog and changed herself into a Waterlily.

"When she comes to pull me up, that is when I change back, and pull *her* down. And then, I shall have a fine feast," Toad Woman laughed and smacked her lips.

The Nipmuc Girl from Wabbaquassett was tired, but she would not give up. Okummus was counting on her. She made her way back to the Swamp, once more.

She looked around, preparing herself for Toad Woman. Her sharp eyes searched through the darkness. Toad Woman was nowhere in sight. The Girl then gave a sigh of relief and turned her focus to the Water.

There it was, the Waterlily; gracefully floating above the murky waters. The Girl walked toward it. She had no idea that it was really the Toad Woman. Toad Woman thought to herself, 'This time, I will catch this troublesome child and eat her up.'

As the Girl stood over the Waterlily, she reached down by her side and pulled out the leather pouch that contained the sap.

Toad Woman was about to change back into her true self. Just then, the Girl broke open the glob of sap and poured it all over the Waterlily. "There, just like Okummus told me," she said. She reached down to pluck it from the Water.

This is when Toad Woman made her move. Or, at least she tried to and came to a horrifying realization.

The Pine Tree sap stuck so firmly to the Waterlily that she could not transform. Toad Woman could not move. She squirmed, struggled, and tried with all her strength, but the sticky layer would not allow her Magic to work. Toad Woman was sealed inside the Waterlily. The girl plucked up the Plant with great delight. She rushed back to her Wigwam.

"I have the Waterlily!" The Girl shouted, as she entered the lodge, "And I poured on the sap, just as you asked."

"Well done, my Dear," the old Lady said.

Okummus had a pot of water boiling over a fire, in the middle of the Wigwam.

"Quick, drop it in." The Grandmother said, "This Waterlily tea and sap will heal my ailment."

The Plant was dropped in the pot. It was boiled, then simmered, until the Waterlily was completely dissolved. The Grandmother drank it all. By the dawn, Okummus was sick no more. She was feeling much stronger and better than ever. Okummus even regained her sight.

—ɯ—

"Crow, those were very pleasing stories," said Bear, "I truly enjoyed them, especially Toad Woman. Was that the end of Toad Woman? And Okummus? Did she not know?"

"That is another Story, Netomp (friend)." Crow replied, "But I am feeling much relieved, now. I shall share a Story, of another Trickster and our confrontation."

Crow Challenges Hobomook

*L*ong ago, it was this way. The Trickster, known to the Nipmuc people as Hobomook, decided he was going to have some fun.

He was going to play some cruel jokes on the Nipmucs. It was during the Summer Berry Harvest that Hobomook decided to start his mischief on a group of Nipmucs that were out in the Forest.

The Human Beings were gathering a delicious variety blueberry, raspberry, strawberry and other seasonal treats, filling their baskets. They had been laboring hard all day, scouting through the Woods for miles to collect only the finest fruits. Once all the baskets were full, they took a brief rest before heading back to the village.

When the Nipmucs were not looking, Hobomook touched their baskets of goods as he chanted a curse. His touch transformed all the sweet goods into small hard stones. He then ran, hid behind a Tree, and peeked out from the side. When the Nipmucs realized what had happened, they were very upset. Some were shouting, wondering who could do such a mean thing. Others cried and were saddened for all of their hard work had been for nothing. Hobomook sat behind the Tree, laughing so hard, that his belly jiggled.

Back at the village, a Woman was cooking a big pot of delicious Rabbit stew. Once it was done, she went inside the Wetu to gather her family to come eat. When the Lady went inside, Hobomook touched the pot then ran off. When the family came out to eat, they were shocked and disgusted. Hobomook had changed the tasty soup into a kettle of boiling mud. The Lady wept for that was the last of the meat. Hobomook was now rolling around on the ground, laughing, and kicking his feet together.

Then there was a young Warrior, carving a new bow from ash wood. It was a sturdy and fine bow, about six feet long. It was meticulously etched with pretty designs of flowers and Birds. The Warrior walked away for a moment to sharpen his carving knife. That is when Hobomook grabbed the bow. The fine bow was changed into dead Willow grass. When the Man returned to continue his work, he looked at his bow in disbelief. His mouth dropped open. His eyes became glazed over with anger. He then shouted out and shook his fist in the air. He had worked on that special bow for weeks. When Hobomook saw how upset the Man was, it made him laugh with even greater delight. Hobomook chuckled and danced around a Tree with his hands on his hips.

Not far from the village were the large Cornfields. There were several Women, of all ages, gathering Corn and singing songs. As they sang and chatted amongst themselves, they filled the large baskets full of ripe and scrumptious Corn. After all the work was done, the Ladies decided to go get a drink. They left their baskets of Corn in the fields and headed down by the stream. That's when Hobomook did it, again.

He went up and down the rows dancing, and smiling, as he touched each basket of Corn. He turned every sweet and tender ear of Corn into a pile of gross fish bones. The entire harvest was gone. When the Women returned from the stream, they were horrified. They yelled and sobbed, while some held their faces in anguish. They went back to the village with their baskets full of only fish skeletons to show for all of their hard work.

A meeting was called by the Sachem. The people gathered at the Longhouse. The Nipmucs were bitter for now they knew this was the handiwork of Hobomook. The Human Beings became extremely angry and wanted to get rid of Hobomook. However, him being a Trickster, he could be very dangerous to tangle with. They asked the Pau Wau, or who we know today as Medicine Man, what should be done.

While they were in their meeting, Konkontu, The Crow was making his daily trip to the Cornfield. The Nipmucs always shared corn with Crow because he is the one who brought it to them, in the first place. The Crow is a very special creature as a Bird that lives between life, death, and Dreams. He also has the mystical power to change form. When Crow reached the Cornfield, he shuddered. He saw that all the tasty Corn was gone. Where all the delicious Corn should be, were now just rows and rows of fish bones.

Konkontu began circling the Cornfield. The more he looked, the angrier he became. He then landed on a large rock. He tilted his head side to side, opened his wings wide, and let out an enormous "CAW!" It was so loud, that it split the boulder down the middle, as he flew off. This time Hobomook went too far. By ruining the Corn, he upset the one creature that could challenge his powers.

Crow flew to the village. He flew inside the Longhouse and circled the people four times. The Crow swooped down and whispered into the ear of the Pau Wau. "What did he say? What did he say?" The people asked. The Pau Wau replied, "Crow said he is very angry with Hobomook, too, for causing such mischief. He is most troubled by the loss of Corn.

Crow said he cannot undo Hobomook's spells. But, he says that we should leave Hobomook for him to deal with and that it's too risky for us. Crow said he will deal with Hobomook another way."

Crow went looking for Hobomook. He found him lying comfortably, down by the River with a look of satisfaction on his face. Crow cawed to him and said, "Hobomook! You have been making great troubles with the Human Beings, I see." Hobomook laughed and said, "Yes, just a little, and I am just getting started. I intend to cause them even more trouble."

"Well, why don't you forget about them and let's have some real fun," said Crow.

"What do you have in mind, that could give me more joy, than harassing the Nipmuc?" Asked Hobomook.

"I challenge you to a Shape Shift contest," dared Crow.

"Shape Shift contest? You could never beat me," laughed Hobomook.

"Well, let us find out if what you say is true," urged Crow.

"Very well Crow, you asked for it. But we must bet something," stated Hobomook.

"I am glad you said that," Crow added, "If I win, you have to change the Human Being's food and other goods back to, as they were."

"Yes, and what do I get if I win?" Inquired Hobomook.

Crow explained, "I will tell you a great secret. A secret that only a creature that travels under the light of the Sun and within the realm of death and Dreams knows. A secret that will add to your ability to Shape Shift, and change, like never before. A secret that goes beyond the winding Rivers and white-tipped Mountains. A secret that is deeper than that of the root of an Oak. A secret that will—" "Enough!" Said Hobomook, "I am convinced, say no more… Please, say no more. I accept this challenge," Hobomook complied.

Hobomook was very curious to know this secret. He figured if it could increase his power, he can then cause even more trouble. "We have an accord Let's do it!" Excitedly said Hobomook. Crow confirms, "Yes, the challenge is on!" Crow's first thought was to get Hobomook away from the village. "To make it more interesting, we will battle as we race to the Great Mountain on the other side of the Winding River."

Crow held out his wings, spun around, and transformed into a large Black Bear. He ran heading Northwest towards the Great Mountain, that we refer to as the *'Berkshires.'* Hobomook laughed, bent over, shimmied his shoulders and changed into Wolf. They darted through the Forest, whizzing in and out, from behind Trees, large rocks, and brush. Glimpses of light and shadow skirted across their bodies. Bear landed his big front paws on huge flat Stone. When his back paws hit the flat Stone, he leaped and changed to Rabbit. Wolf sees a large log out in front. As he jumps over it, he changes to Deer.

"Hey Crow, watch this," Hobomook yelled, as he turned into Raccoon.

"CAW!" Said Crow, "You better watch out!" Crow changed into a huge Moose and charged at full steam, nearly trampling the Raccoon. Hobomook shrieked as the giant hoof came near. He quickly changed into a Groundhog and went underground. He popped out nearby coming out the other end as a Rattlesnake.

He saw the Moose getting distance and transformed into Cougar. He stretched out his Cat body and dashed forward. Cougar caught up to the Moose and they ran side, by side.

They reach the River Connecticut. The Moose leaped for the Water. He changed into a Salmon, in midair. Cougar jumped straight up high in the air and changed to a large Sturgeon. They swam for the other side of the River. Salmon leaped up and changed into a Black Hawk. Sturgeon burst high above the Water and changed into Turkey Vulture.

They flew high in the air towards the Mountain, swerving in and out of each other. They sliced through clouds, as the wind lifted their wings on high. They came across a flock of Geese who hurriedly got out of their way, as they zipped through the middle of the formation.

They landed at the top of the Mountain, as they continued to alter themselves. Now, they changed back and forth at a greater pace: Crow into Turtle, Hobomook into Dragonfly. The Dragonfly buzzed to a Tree branch and hung upside down. Hobomook then changed into Bat. Turtle began growing large square front teeth, as he turned into Beaver. Hobomook grabbed a handful of Pine needles from the ground and said, "Watch this!" He dropped them over his head and changed into a Porcupine.

Back and forth they went. A fierce rainstorm came with gusting winds. The two of them continued on, through the harsh Storm. Through wind and rain, the battle went on for days, and days. They were both very tired but neither would quit.

"Are you running out of things to change into, Crow?" Taunted Hobomook.

"No. Are you getting tired, Hobomook?" Asked Crow.

"Not at all!" Replied Hobomook.

But then abruptly, Crow changed back to himself. He stopped changing and stood there with his head down. Hobomook looked at him. A grin came over his face. Hobomook shouted with glee, "Hah! I won! You are done, I defeated you!"

Crow did not say a word. He continued to stand there with his beak pointed down.

Hobomook locked his hands behind his back and danced and danced. He danced and laughed some more.

Then he ran over to Crow and said, "Crow, I won. Now, tell me this great secret." Crow gave him a kind glance, and said, "Well, I really shouldn't."

"You tell me, Crow, you tell me now!" Hobomook demanded. Crow said, "Very well. The secret is: that the biggest change we can make to ourselves will never come from the outside. The biggest change comes only from the inside. When we first started this battle, I was very angry with you. I wanted revenge. But as these days went on, I decided to forgive you. Therefore, I changed my anger into great compassion. My compassion toward you and forgiveness in my heart made me want to let you win."

Hobomook was utterly stunned. Then he became embarrassed. Then he got even angrier than before, and exclaimed, "Noooo! You cannot do this to me! Not fair! You have to battle!"

"I am," said Crow, "This was my final change: Compassion."

"Oh yeah! Well, I can still beat you, Crow. I refuse to let you outdo me! I will change into even bigger compassion!" Yelled Hobomook.

"Watch this! I will show you, Crow! I will show big, big compassion!" Assured Hobomook. He then went back to the Nipmuc village. Hobomook returned all the items back to the way they were. The many baskets that were once tainted by Hobomook, were now filled with all those wonderful goods, fruits, and Berries. The big pot of savory and delicious Rabbit stew was back inside the Wetu. The beautifully-carved, ash bow was returned to the young Warrior. Lastly, the Cornfields, and baskets of the fresh, and delicious Corn, were now restored. This made the Pau Wau and all the Nipmuc people very happy and also filled them with much gratitude.

Hobomook laughed triumphantly, and proudly, "There Crow, I showed even bigger compassion. Outdo that!"

Crow replied, "Yes, Hobomook. It would seem you have defeated me."

—ɷ—

"Ah, Crow, you are wise—and crafty, I might say!" Bear voiced. "It would seem you recall the many talents you possess. Have you found your Dream?"

Crow stood firm, beheld the Forest all around. "I have found," he replied, "A good friend in you, Bear."

Bear smiled and nodded.

Crow gazed up to the Sky. A sense of joy came over him.

"What do you see?" Asked Bear.

"Bear, I want to tell you a very special Story," Said Crow. "It is about how my Clan came to this World. I remember it all, now."

How Crow Brought the Corn

*L*ong ago, a terrible crisis fell upon the people of Nipmuc.

It was a dry, hot summer and food supplies were running short. There were too few Animals to hunt, and the Rivers and Lakes were too shallow to fish. The moaning of empty stomachs echoed across the Land. Looking for answers, they went to the Clan Mother Okummus, who was also a Pau Wau.

A Nipmuc Man pleaded with the Medicine Woman, "Okummus, can you do something? There are no Sachems, no Warriors, nobody to find an answer to this dilemma and stop the suffering."

The Elder did the only thing she could do, that was to go into the *Dreamworld* to find an answer.

After much prayer, a visionary dream came to the Pau Wau. *There is a powerful Seed in the Heart of the Sun. This Seed will surely nourish all of your*

Nation and many more, to come," The *Dream* told her. If she could now retrieve this Seed, her people would be saved.

'But who could go to the mighty, and powerful Sun?' She pondered.
A Great Council came together to discuss this matter. The Nipmucs even
counseled with all the creatures of the Forest. For the Animals were very
sad for their Two-Legged Brothers and Sisters, and wanted to help, too.

Human, Animal, Birds, Insects, and all others of the Woodland joined
in a huge Circle. Okummus shared her Dream. All of them listened very
carefully. It was decided that someone must go to the Sun. Since Human
Beings could not fly, they were not a good choice. So, Aohkeaumoous
(Bumble Bee) volunteered to go. "I will fly to the Sun. I will carry the Seed
in my pollen basket," she said.

Off Bumble Bee went, on her journey to reach the Sun. She flew with
fearless determination, but the Sun was very far away. Her small wings
became too tired to go on. And the Sky became too hot for her to endure.
She was forced to turn back. When Bumble Bee returned to the Circle,
her body had turned yellow and some parts were black from the Sun's hot
rays.

Since Bumble Bee could not make it, Owl went to the middle of the
Circle, and said, "*I*, will fly to the Sun and retrieve the Seed. My wings
are much larger than Bumble Bee." Owl stated proudly, "Surely, I will
succeed." Owl quickly took flight with his large, strong wings, husking
through the air.

He headed straight for the Sun. Owl flew much closer than Bumble
Bee. But the pure brightness of the Sun was too much for him to endure. He was forced to turn away. But, not before injuring his eyes. After
that day, he became far sighted, which means he cannot see things up
close very well. Owl was upset, and went before the Council, "I do not

think this journey can be accomplished. The Sun is too bright, and too far away." The people of the village were sad and beginning to lose all hope.

That is when another Bird stepped before the Council. His name was Ketookau. He was large and completely snow white in color. This beautiful white bird was known to be an elegant speaker, with a smooth voice. Ketookau addressed the Council, "I recognize the dilemma before my Two-Legged Brothers and Sisters. I'm truly delighted with sharing the Forest with the Human Beings, therefore, I will bestow my assistance onto this Council and retrieve the Seed." The Medicine Woman nodded.

Ketookau continued to speak, "I have always been quite pleased with getting any kind of Seed. They are all good, you know," he said, as he turned to Owl.

"When I was just a small bird, I would sit by the stream, waiting to catch some windblown Seeds from Willow, or Acorn, or Chestnut, or—"

"Ketookau," said Owl, "Remember your task? The Sun?"

"Certainly, I do, Owl." Ketookau replied. "But, assuredly, there is always time to share a few words amongst friends. Like the time I was flying from—"

"Ketookau!" Owl shouted, "Stop talking and start flying!"

The Nipmucs were very grateful for Ketookau offering his help. However, there was a lot of fear and doubt amongst the Human Beings and the Animals. They didn't think he had a chance. The Pau Wau decided to do a special Ceremony for Ketookau.

Pau Wau gathered up some Tree and Stone Medicine. She collected dried herbs of Sage, Sweet Grass, Cedar, and Tobacco. She took a small amount of the mix and made a tiny bundle. She told Ketookau to take the bundle as protection.

When all the other Animals of the Forest saw what the Pau Wau had done, they did the same for Ketookau.

Each creature prepared a small bundle of their own Sacred Medicine: Bear, Loon, Rabbit, Beaver, Wolf, Spider, Turtle, and so on. Ketookau strung all the bundles together and wrapped them around his neck. He thanked them all, for their gifts. He chatted some more and then was underway. The large white Bird set off to the Sun to get the lifesaving Seed that came to the Pau Wau in a Dream.

He flew, and flew, until he could no longer be seen in the Sky. Nightfall came and Ketookau had not returned. The next day arrived and he was not back. A few days went by, and still no Ketookau. Two weeks passed, and there was still no sign of him. Most of the Human Beings and Animals had stopped waiting, fearing he was dead. Sadness and despair were growing, even greater. The Nipmucs felt he was their last hope, but he must have failed.

But the Medicine Woman, weak and weary, herself, never gave up and never turned her eyes away from the Sky. She watched and waited. The following day, the Pau Wau looked to the Western Sky. She noticed something coming over the horizon. It looked like a dot in the sky. She rubbed her tired eyes and looked again. A big, shiny, black Bird came into focus. It was coming from the direction of the Setting Sun. It soared closer, and closer, with its dark wings, thrashing through the air.

As the black Bird circled over her head, she could see it had something in its beak. It was the Seed. The Seed in her Dream, from the Sun. The black Bird landed next to the Pau Wau. He placed the Seed on the ground and stood in silence.

The Pau Wau was confused because she knew Ketookau was white.

"Ketookau? Is that you?" She asked.

The bird did not quickly respond. It looked around.

Then, in a deep, gravelly voice he said, "Ketookau? Ketookau? Ah yes, I remember. But now, I am Konkontu, the Crow. I have flown into the realm between life, death and Dreams. The immense power of Father Sun has forever parched my smooth voice, and blackened my white feathers as dark as the night sky. I would have surely died, but it was the Medicine from all the different Animals, Trees, and Human Beings, that kept me going, during this extremely difficult journey. Each of you now live within me. Now, and forever, I will fly in realms between life, death, and Dreams. But, you, my Sister, your Tribe shall live. For your Dream was correct. This Seed that I pulled from the Sun, shall keep you alive and nourish you all for many generations to come."

The Elder fell to her knees with gratitude.

"And because I paid such a price to retrieve this Seed," Crow said, "I will come, from time to time, to eat of this Seed."

The Pau Wau agreed and thanked him, once more.

The Nipmuc people called the Seed, *'Weatchimin.'*

The English had never seen Weatchimin, prior to first contact. When they arrived on Turtle Island, they named it 'Corn.'

—m—

"My Brother Crow, the bringer of such a tasty treat," said Bear. "You have shared some of the most interesting Stories. But have you found your Dream?" He asked.

Crow looked up to the Sky. Bear did, also.

A tremendous roar of Thunder boomed.

Off in the distance, they saw several clouds quickly coming together.

The clouds swelled and churned.

They grew darker and more massive.

Amidst the thunder, lighting, and wind; the enormous black clouds moved at great speed across the Sky. They began to slow, just as it hovered above Crow and Bear.

Another Earth-shaking crash of Thunder shook the black clouds.

An enormous Lightning bolt hit through the center of it.

The clouds cracked in many places. Then it shattered into small pieces, like shiny, black arrowheads.

These portions began to tumble and spin toward the Earth. As each piece twirled down, it transformed into a Crow.

The Sky began to fill with thousands of Crows, charging straight down.

They were heading for Crow and Bear.

They swooped down and formed a magnificent column.

Just before reaching Crow and Bear, the shot back up, and to the West.

As this massive gathering of Crows flew by, Bear's fur fluttered from the strong gust. Crow's feathers under his neck ruffled, and the wind beneath his wings beckoned him to join.

The Birds opened a spot for Crow to take his place in the formation.

Crow looked at Bear, smiled and said, "Thank you Brother."

Bear beamed back and nodded.

Crow shot up into the Sky.

He circled Bear four times, then soared up, where he took his place, amongst his Clan.

Bear watched as his friend flew away. He watched and waited.

He waited until the last Crow was out of view.

The Sky went calm, clear, and quiet again.
Bear picked up his Drum and walked back to the edge of Fresh Water
Lake.
He gazed across the pond.
The warm Sun began to set, just below the edge of the Water.
The twilight mist hovered silently above.
A leaping Trout splashed up and gulped a Water bug.

The End

Keep Drumming & Dreaming

CrowStormPublishing2017®

About the Author

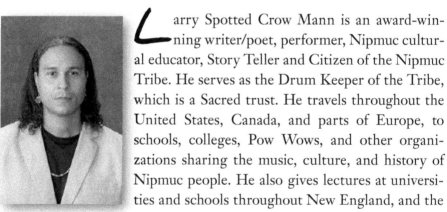

*L*arry Spotted Crow Mann is an award-winning writer/poet, performer, Nipmuc cultural educator, Story Teller and Citizen of the Nipmuc Tribe. He serves as the Drum Keeper of the Tribe, which is a Sacred trust. He travels throughout the United States, Canada, and parts of Europe, to schools, colleges, Pow Wows, and other organizations sharing the music, culture, and history of Nipmuc people. He also gives lectures at universities and schools throughout New England, and the United States, on issues ranging from Native American sovereignty, to identity.

In 2010, his poetry won a competition in the Memescapes Journal of Fine Arts. In 2013, his poetry was nominated for the Pushcart Prize. *Mann's Tales from the Whispering* Basket is an Internationally-acclaimed and compelling collection of short stories and poetry that has received excellent reviews. His ground-breaking novel, *The Mourning Road to Thanksgiving* won the 2015 WordCraft Circle of Native American Writers Award.

Among his other important work, Mann has worked in collaboration with the Massachusetts Department of Public Health in creating the booklet *"Coming Home: A Guide to Help in the Prevention and Treatment of Substance Abuse of Native American Youth."* And the follow up book: *Circle Tied to Mother Earth* Mann contributed to the book *"Stories of Educational Journeys: Indigenous - Learning & Socio-Cultural Approach in Education"* by Kathleen Noyes, Ed.D.

Mann was applauded for his role in the PBS Native American film, *"We Shall Remain,"* directed by Chris Eyre.

Also featured in two documentaries and Winner of the NPS 2007 Award for Interpretive Media *"Living in Two Worlds: Native American Experiences on the Boston Harbor Islands,"* and *"First Patriots,"* produced by Aaron Cadieux.

Most recently, Mann was featured in X-MEN- The New Mutants, directed by Josh Boone, due to be released April 2018

Furthermore, Mann has worked in the field of Human Services for over 13 years, mostly in the field of Mental Health and helping our at-risk youth.

Published materials Include:

* Poetry in *"Memescapes Journal of Fine Arts"* at Quinsigamond College
* Various Articles in Indian Country Today Magazine
* Contributing Work in the Book *"New England on Fire,"* by Margaret Barton,
* *"Native American Anthology of New England:* Dawn Land Voices University of Nebraska Press
* Charles River Journal

* Go Green Conference for the Medical Services Administration of Puerto Rico
* WordCraft Circle of Native American Writers
* *"My Heart Is Red Project: A Journey Across the United States and Canada,"* Photography and Video of Native Americans, by Mayoke Photography

For more information or to order a book go to:
www.whisperingbasket.com

CPSIA information can be obtained
at www.ICGtesting.com
Printed in the USA
FFHW02n1722300818
48184234-51903FF